Understanding
The Israelite-Samaritans
From Ancient to Modern

An Introductory Atlas

BENYAMIM TSEDAKA

First published in 2017 by
CARTA Jerusalem

Editor: Lorraine Kessel
Maps & Graphics: Carta, Jerusalem

Picture Sources:
Photographs are by Ori Orhof & from Wikimedia Commons, in the public domain, and have been attributed to their authors.
All other illustrations are from the archives of Carta, Jerusalem.

Carta Jerusalem, Ltd.
11 Rivka Street, P.O.B. 2500,
Jerusalem 9102401, Israel
E-mail: carta@carta.co.il
www.carta-jerusalem.com

ISBN: 978-965-220-888-0

Printed in the United States of America

CONTENTS

The Kingdoms of Israel and Judah - The Divided Kingdom

10th Century BCE

And he said to Jeroboam, Take thee ten pieces: for thus saith the LORD, the God of Israel, Behold, I will rend the kingdom out of the hand of Solomon, and will give ten tribes to thee:

I Kings: 11 31

And Rehoboam went to Shechem: for to Shechem were all Israel come to make him king.

II Chronicles 10:1

1. General History

The Israelite-Samaritans are the remnant of an ancient people, descended from the ancient kingdom of Israel, whose attempts to achieve peace among the people of Israel were rejected by the leaders of the descendants of the kingdom of Judah, the Israelite Jews. In general, historical research of the people of Israel tends to see the Samaritans as a sect that split off from Judaism in the Second Temple period (538 BCE - 70 CE), adopting in this period a version of the Pentateuch with features differing from the Jewish Masoretic text of the Pentateuch. This widespread view is derived from a patronizing attitude in Biblical research that prioritizes Judaism to the Samaritans. As a wiseman said: "The winners always write the history."

Moreover, studies of the history of the Israelite-Samaritan people that initially make a connection between them and the foreigners brought in by the emperors of Assyria pretend to be objective, but actually spread disinformation about the Israelite-Samaritans. It is obvious from books 2 Kings and 2 Chronicles in the Bible and from archaeological excavations that the link suggested in the Second Temple period by Jewish Sages as a result of the great polemic between the Jews and Samaritans should be disregarded.

In fact, the Israelite-Samaritans and those foreigners were two different groups. The Israelite-Samaritans continued the northern Israelite lineage and heritage while the foreigners were brought in to administer the Assyrian colonies in place of the Israelite elite in the kingdom of Israel, while the majority of the northern Israelites remained on their lands in Samaria after the Assyrian conquest.

The discovery of the Dead Sea Scrolls in the Judean Desert, especially many of the scrolls found in Qumran Cave No. 4, revealed scrolls of the Pentateuch written by Jews who had abandoned their urban life for an independent life in the desert in the last two centuries BCE and the first century CE. Some sections of these scrolls are either identical or closely resemble the text of the Israelite-Samaritan version of the Pentateuch and differ somewhat from the Jewish Masoretic text. This fact leads one to the conclusion that in ancient times there were different versions of the Pentateuch, some written and passed on from generation to generation in the north of the land of Israel, the original home of the Israelite-Samaritans; and some written in the south of the land of Israel, forming the Jewish Masoretic text of the Pentateuch.

The main difference between Judaism and Samaritanism concerns the matter of the sacred center: the Temple Mount in Judaism and Mount Gerizim in Samaritanism. This difference began with the different geographical origin of the two groups that became two different nations.

The Hill of Samaria

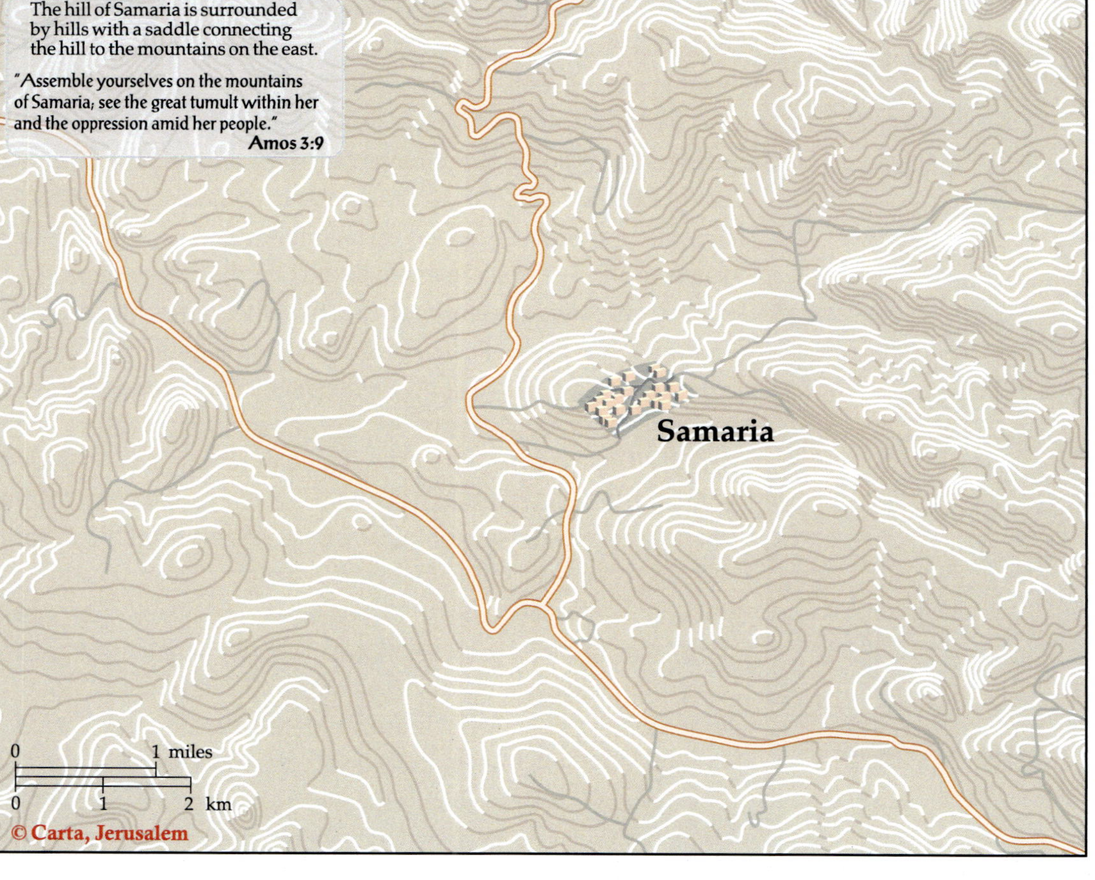

The hill of Samaria is surrounded by hills with a saddle connecting the hill to the mountains on the east.

"Assemble yourselves on the mountains of Samaria; see the great tumult within her and the oppression amid her people."
Amos 3:9

The Temple Mount is located at the heart of the region of Judea, the foundation of the Jewish culture (the term Jew is derived from the region of Judea). Mount Gerizim is located at the heart of the region of Samaria, the foundation of the Israelite-Samaritan culture (the term Samaritan is derived from the region of Samaria).

There can be no greater mistake than to consider the Israelite-Samaritans as a sect which split off from the main Jewish stream in Judaism. In its early phase in the Second Temple period there were many sects in Judaism such as the Pharisees, Sadducees, Essenes and others, but none of these sects was similar in structure and characteristics to the Israelite-Samaritans.

The Israelite-Samaritans,

descendants of the Israelites who lived in the kingdom of Israel and in the north of the Land of Israel, had their own territory, the land of Samaria, and they also spread in large numbers to the plains in the north and south, had governors and kings, possessed armies that rebelled against foreign rulers, and followed a way of life based solely on the commandments of the Pentateuch.

In the Byzantine period (295-634 CE) there were at least nine sects that split off from the mainstream of the Israelite-Samaritans and generally known as Dositheans. Some of them survived until the end of the 10th century CE.

If it is claimed that the Israelite-Samaritans were part of Judaism, they would surely have consecrated other books and scrolls apart from the Pentateuch, as the Jews did, but the Pentateuch remains the sole sacred book of the Israelite-Samaritans.

On the contrary, historical research shows that so-called normative Judaism was a development of one of the leading sects in Judaism in its early stages, the Pharisees, and rejected the other sects. This development left only the two main streams of Judaism: the Jewish Karaites, who accepted the entire Bible and rejected the later literature, and the rabbinic Jews, who adopted and consecrated the Bible and the Mishnah and Talmud, the oral Torah.

The Israelite-Samaritan tradition based on the Pentateuch is the most ancient biblical tradition, while the Jewish-Karaite tradition based on the entire Bible and the Jewish rabbinic tradition based on the whole Bible plus the post-biblical literature such as the Mishnah and Talmud and other works, both represent later traditions.

Another common mistake in biblical scholarship and the historiography of the people of Israel is to make a connection

Selection of ivories from the royal palace in Samaria
From the archives of Carta, Jerusalem

Portion of the Temple Scroll, one of the longest of the Dead Sea Scrolls.
2nd century BCE
Source: The Israel Museum's 'Dead Sea Scrolls Digital Project'
Author: Israel Museum
Via Wikimedia Commons

between the Israelite-Samaritans and the foreign tribes brought in by the Assyrians to administer the Assyrian colonies in Judea, Samaria, Galilee and Edom. These foreigners were brought in to replace the elite of the destroyed kingdom of Israel exiled from the country by the rulers of the Assyrian Empire and to administer the colonies for the benefit of the Assyrian Empire. All of them were settled in administrative cities like Samaria, Gezer etc., followed their pagan customs and worshipped their gods. On the other hand, most of the Israelites of the destroyed Kingdom of Israel remained on their lands and continued to pay taxes to the Assyrian rulers collected by the newcomers.

The massive presence of the Israelites after the Assyrian conquest has been attested to by many excavations and surveys conducted since 1967, and whose results have been published in many articles. The continuity of the ancient Israelites in the north of the country, and the Israelite-Samaritans on Mount Gerizim in later periods, is shown by the excavations of the ancient Samaritan city of Luza, which existed from the Persian period to the end of the Hellenistic period. These excavations revealed over 500 stone inscriptions and masses of cultic implements that leave no doubt that the ancient Israelites and their successors the Israelite-Samaritans maintained a monotheistic cult throughout the entire period and were not influenced by pagan symbols or by pagan worship.

The creation of a linkage between the Israelite-Samaritans and paganism and/or pagan tribes has a tendency to cast doubt on the sources of their culture. However, eminent scholars of the Bible and of the history of the people of Israel have stated that the Israelite-Samaritans are descendants of the ancient Israelite people of the kingdom of Israel.

In the fourth and fifth centuries CE, the Israelite-Samaritans numbered about 1,500,000 people living in various towns and villages in the country, from southern Syria to northern Egypt. Cruel religious decrees, forced conversions to Christianity and Islam, massacres and persecutions, thinned the Samaritan community to a mere 141 people by 1919.

In the 1930s the community reached a turning-point and began to increase. Since then, the community has been gradually developing in all areas of life. In addition to being the smallest and one of the oldest peoples in the world, they are also the youngest community, according to the average age of its members. In 2017 the community numbered 420 in Holon, south of Tel-Aviv, Israel, and 380 in Kiryat Luza, Mount Gerizim, Samaria.

2. The Samaritans in Shechem [Nablus] and on Mount Gerizim and in Holon

11 And Moses charged the people the same day, saying,
12 These shall stand upon mount Gerizim to bless the people, when ye are come over Jordan; Simeon, and Levi, and Judah, and Issachar, and Joseph, and Benjamin:
13 And these shall stand upon mount Ebal to curse; Reuben, Gad, and Asher, and Zebulun, Dan, and Naphtali

Deuteronomy. 27: 11-13

Remains of a Samaritan Building from the Hellenistic Period on Mount Gerizim
Photo from:The New Encyclopedia of Archaeological Excavations in the Holy Land: Vol. 2, p. 457

The Samaritans are descendants of the inhabitants of the ancient kingdom of Israel which split off from the kingdom of Judah after the death of King Solomon who, together with his father, maintained a united kingdom for seventy years up to the year 930 BCE. The Samaritans are named after the central region and capital of the kingdom of Israel, Samaria. Their traditional name: "Shaamerem" means "Keepers" – who preserve the true Israelite tradition based on the five books of the Torah of Moses.

The kingdom of Israel sometimes cooperated with the kingdom of Judah, and sometimes the two kingdoms fought each other. The struggle between them led to the fall of the kingdom of Israel to the Assyrians. The kingdom of Judah asked the Assyrian empire for aid against the alliance of the kingdom of Israel with the chief power in the area, Aram. The Assyrians conquered the kingdom of Israel and exiled the elite of the Israelite population to Assyria. As a result of this conquest, most of the conquered population had to pay taxes to the Assyrians. The Babylonians continued this system when they conquered the kingdom of Judah. Until the conquest of the two kingdoms, the inhabitants of the kingdom of Israel were called "men of Israel" and the inhabitants of the kingdom of Judah were called "men of Judah."

The Israelites who remained in the country after the Assyrian conquest included among them part of the foreign elite which the Assyrians brought to Samaria. Those who were not

Assyrian Attacks on Israel and Judah; 724-721 BCE

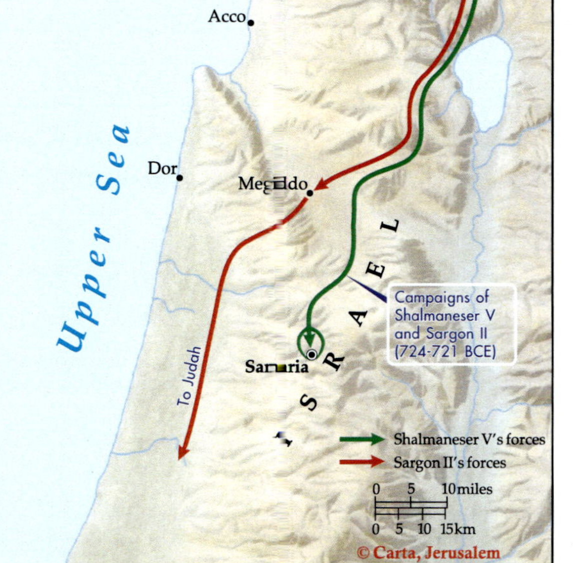

The Exile of Peoples to and from Israel under the Assyrians; 738-712 BCE

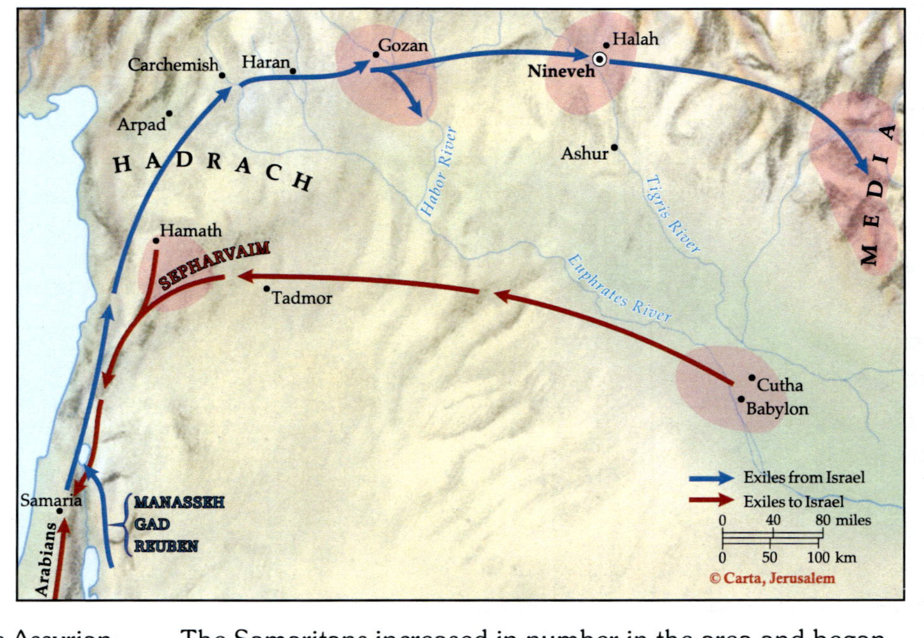

absorbed returned to their country after the fall of the Assyrian and Babylonian empires The Israelite majority continued to grow and to spread in Samaria and the other Assyrian provinces until a small part of the Judeans returned from Babylon at the beginning of the Persian conquest.

Attempts to unite the two parts of the Israelite people at the beginning of the period of Persian rule under the leadership of those who returned from Babylon failed. Ezra and Nehemiah (who returned after seven generations in exile, from 586 BCE to 428 BCE), brought with them the special Judean culture which had been created in exile It was not suited to life in the country and the two elements diverged, especially as the majority of the Israelites who remained in the area did not wish to accept the overlordship of the Judean minority that had returned from Babylon.

Thus, towards the end of the 4th century BCE, the two parts of the people of Israel crystallized as two separate bodies: one part was called Judeans after Judah and the other part was called Samaritans after Samaria The Samaritans chose Shechem as their center, and the capital of the kingdom of Israel became a Greek-Hellenistic city. Around Mount Gerizim, their unique tradition based on the Torah of Moses flourished, while the Judeans, clustered around Jerusalem, based their tradition on their version of the Torah and the Oral Law which their sages created in order to interpret the written Torah.

In Shechem, the Samaritan people began to develop. The Judeans sometimes fought the Samaritans and sometimes the two entities cooperated against a common enemy. It should be noted that times of hostility exceeded times of cooperation because of their differing ideologies. Samaritans claimed Mount Gerizim as the holy center, whereas Judeans claimed the Temple Mount in Jerusalem as the holy center.

In 69 CE the Roman emperor Titus founded a new city called Neapolis next to ancient Shechem, west of Mount Gerizim and Mount Ebal.

The Samaritans increased in number in the area and began to spread westwards from Shechem and Samaria to areas like the Galilee, the Beit Shean Valley, the Mediterranean coast and the southern Negev. Samaritan settlements developed east of the Jordan in the Golan Heights and in Gilead. At their numerical peak in the 5th century CE they numbered more than a million and a half inhabitants. This number is based on the losses incurred by the Samaritans in their rebellions against Byzantine rule, which aimed at their conversion to Christianity, in 484, 529 and 556 CE.

This number included the Samaritan settlements which developed in Tyre and Sidon and in the centers of the powers that ruled the area over the years: in Shushan (Susa), the capital of Persia, in Athens and Thessalonica, on the island of Delos in Greece, in Rome, in Sicily, in Alexandria, in Upper Egypt, and in the islands of the Mediterranean and the Reed Sea. Scholars estimate the Samaritan population in the diaspora at 150,000 individuals, but the center of the Samaritan people was and remains Shechem throughout the generations. At the head of the people stood the high priest from the family of Pinhas ben Elazar ben Aharon, the brother of Moses. Priests in other cities were subordinate to him, as were the leaders of the Samaritan army, which had a number of successes in the struggle against Rome.

The great age of the Samaritans in Shechem and Neapolis was the 4th century CE. In addition to the military successes, there was a flowering of Samaritan culture, ceremonial orders were fixed in Shechem and new synagogues were built. In the Shechem area and in the surrounding villages schools were established for the study of the religion. This period of flowering in the 4th century lasted for three generations.

But the major defeats of the Samaritans in their rebellions against the Byzantines at the end of the 5th century and during the 6th century CE diminished the strength of the Samaritan people, and it lost four-fifths of its numbers. Thus, the Samaritans at the beginning of the 7th century on the eve of the coming of the Muslims to the area numbered about 300,000.

At the beginning of the Arab conquest, the Samaritans were concentrated in two areas: in Transjordan in the east and in Palestine [As it called by the Romans] in the west. The Samaritans in Transjordan collaborated with the Arab invaders and even served as guides for their armies in their expulsion of the Byzantines. The Samaritans in Palestine, on the other hand, collaborated with the Byzantines, causing heavy casualties among the Samaritans during the Arab conquest of the cities of Caesarea and Gaza. Thirty thousand Samaritans fell in the Caesarea area and five thousand in the Gaza area.

Under Arab rule, Neapolis became Nablus. The successive Muslim regimes – Omayyads, Abbasids and Ayyubids – and the invasion of the area by Mongolian tribes, led to the overthrow of the Samaritan people. Especially under Abbasid rule, the Samaritans experienced harsh religious persecutions and many of them converted to Islam. When Ayyubid rule began, with the defeat of the Crusaders, the Samaritans numbered tens of thousands, and most of those converted to Islam in the Mameluke period.

In reaction to the wave of religious conversions, there was a glorious age of cultural flowering in Nablus from the 13th to the 15th century CE. In those three hundred years, most of the Samaritan works in poetry, Bible commentary, history and reckoning of the Samaritan calendar were written.

Nablus became in the course of time a place of refuge for persecuted Samaritans everywhere. The Damascus community was destroyed in the 17th century and the Gaza and Cairo communities in the 18th century. Stone inscriptions from these communities in various museums and scrolls of the law testify to the richness of their lives. Refugees from these communities came to Nablus to end their lives there. At the end of the 19th century and the beginning of the 20th, the Samaritans in Nablus plus a small family in Jaffa numbered 141 souls, 81 males and 60 females, including only 25 children.

Throughout the generations, in Shechem, Neapolis and Nablus, there has been a high priest from the time of the Exodus until today. The present high priest is the 132nd from Aaron, the brother of Moses. The family of high priests has preserved the existence of the Samaritans throughout the generations and led them in the most difficult of times.

The religious life of the Samaritans is centered around the holy places on the summit of Mount Gerizim: the altar of Abraham and his son Isaac, the stones of the first altar brought by Joshua from the Jordan, and Giv'at Olam (the Hill of Eternity), the holiest place of all, where the tabernacle of Moses stood. In other places, there are the burial-sites of various biblical figures.

With the coming of the British in 1917, the return of the Jews to the land of Israel and the relaxing of political and economic pressures, there was a new flowering of Samaritan life in the area and the development of a second Samaritan community

The Holy Land Under Roman Rule 1st Cent. BCE - 1st Cent CE

in the Jaffa–Tel-Aviv region, and, from 1955, in Holon. south of Tel-Aviv.

The notables of the city of Nablus knew how to honour the Samaritans. The grandfather of the present high priest was a member of the city council for all the 42 years he was in office (1874-1916). His two successors were highly respected by the people of Nablus who saw them as an inseparable part of their city.

After the establishment of the Palestinian Authority, the high priest Shalom Ben Amram became a member of the Palestinian parliament due to the respect that the Palestinians had for the ancient Israelite community, that they regarded as part of their own identity.

But the daily pressure of the Israeli-Palestinian conflict caused the Samaritans damage, whether in property physical, or spiritual. They were obliged to find a place of residence where they could live their lives in relative peace. Thus, in

1998, the last Samaritan left the Samaritan neighborhood in Nablus for a new neighborhood on Mount Gerizim. This new neighborhood was named Kiryat Luza after the ancient city in the Hellenistic period, and after one of the thirteen names of Mount Gerizim. Kiryat Luza is an inseparable part of Nablus. The Samaritans have a great deal of business in Nablus. They have many shops and many of them work in the offices of the Palestinian administration. The inhabitants of Nablus are welcomed guests in Kiryat Luza and many young Samaritans are graduates of the local university.

The Samaritans today – 800 at the beginning of 2017 – have increased more than fivefold in number from their lowest 141, in March 1919. Some 420 live in Holon, south of Tel-Aviv, and the rest on Mount Gerizim. All the families in Holon have built houses on Mount Gerizim where the whole community gathers on Passover, at times of pilgrimage, and on days of festivity and mourning. Despite geographic and political distance, the Samaritans have not ceased to be a single, cohesive community with a common destiny and each cares for the other in every political situation. The Samaritans in Nablus, on Mount Gerizim and in Holon seek peace. A committee set up in Washington and Holon in November 2005 awards the Samaritan peace medal to peace and humanitarian activists throughout the world. In Nablus, the medal has been awarded to previous and present mayors of the city and to the chairmen of the Palestinian Workers' Federation. On the national level, the medal was awarded to the president of the State of Israel, Reuven Rivlin, to the prime minister of Israel, Binyamin Netanyahu, and to the heads of the Palestinian Authority, Salam Fayyad and Rami Hamdallah. They, and others, are regarded as brothers and partners in making peace in the area.

Politically, the Samaritans desire only one thing: peace that will bring economic, cultural, political and social benefits to all people of the area. The Israelite-Samaritans engage in activities of peace and understanding with all political elements in the area and continue to be a bridge of peace between them, for the continued existence of one of the most ancient communities in the world is assured in an atmosphere of peace.

The Spread of Samaritan Settlement in the Mediterranean

3. Israelite-Samaritan Settlements in the 1st & 2nd Millennia CE

In the Land of Israel:

In Samaria:

Shechem, Abarta, Salem, Kiryat Nemara, Karawa, Kiryat Luza, Dabarin, Beit Dajan, Eilon Moreh, Kiryat Mahaneh (Askar), Kafr Kalil, Marda, Beit Bazin, Kafr Hares, 'Asafa, Kiryat Sarin (Ein Mishpat), Ein Ganim (Jenin), Imtin, 'Aqraba, Beit Furiq, Bedan, Tubas, Kafr Sara, Quza, Beit Za'in (Wazan), Barkai, Geva, Safarin, Shomron, Kafr Sila, Tapuah, Hatzerot, Saretan, Shiloh, Ga'ash, Timna, Farata, Beit Rima, Horon, Kefar Kadum, Kafr Naqura, Khirbet Samara

In Galilee:

Tiberias, Safed, Beit Shafat, Samariya (between Acre and Nahariya)

In Beit She'an Valley:

Beit She'an, Farashta, Resifta, Fanutiya, Kafr Qaranim, Tiyasir

In Judean Hills:

Beit Horon, Emaus, Sha'alvim, Jerusalem, Hebron

In the Sharon:

Karkur, Gat, Zeita, Yeshuv, Socho, Tulkarm, Deir El Ghusun, Bil'an, 'Anabta, Kafr Qaqun, Bira, Tayiba, Tzoran, Kfar Saba, Antipatris, Petrus, Lod, Ramla, Safariya, Tzrifin, Beit Dagon

On the coast:

Acre, Haifa, Caesarea, Gedor, Dor, Kafr Fagasha, Arsuf, Haram 'Ali, Galil, Kfar Shalem, Ein Kushi, Jaffa, Yavneh (Yama), Ashkelon (Gerar), Mayumas, Gaza, Rafiah, Hatzerim, Samaritan Island (in the Red Sea)

In eastern Transjordan:

Tarsila, Jebel Vusha, Mt. Nebo, Medeba, Salt, Ajlun

In Mediterranean Countries:

In Syria:

Damascus, Aleppo, Hama

In Lebanon:

Tyre, Sidon, Baalbek

In Egypt:

Yeb, Kafr Samariya, Alexandria, Cairo

In Persia:

Shushan (Susa).

In Greece:

Athens, Thessalonika

In Mediterranean islands:

Delos, Crete, Syracuse, Katania (in Sicily)

In Turkey:

Constantinople (Istanbul)

In Croatia:

Solin.

4. The Israelite-Samaritans – A Small, Special Peace-Loving People

Who are the Israelite-Samaritans?

First we will clarify what they are not.

The Israelite-Samaritans are not Jews, who were first given that name by the Assyrians on account of their origins in Judah. The Israelite-Samaritans are not Samarians, who were first given that name by the Assyrians on account of their origins in Samaria.

The Jews adopted the title and called themselves Jews. The Israelite-Samaritans are Israelites who preserve the truth of the Torah and have not adopted the title "Samarians" which was given to the ancestors of that people only for foreigners to distinguish them from others.

The Israelite-Samaritans are not Palestinians, most of whom are descended from Jews and Samarians who converted to Islam. Not only is this genetically proven by blood and DNA samples of Palestinians, Jews and Samarians, but by the fact that the great Arab cities of the Middle East are full of families of Jewish or Samarian origins. Even the family appointed by the Wakf to guard the Muslim Holy Places in Jerusalem is of Samarian origin.

The Israelite-Samaritans are not Christians and not Muslims, not Druze and not Circassians, not Bahai and not Shiites, not Alawites and not Sunni.

Then, who are the Israelite-Samaritans?

The Israelite-Samaritans are ancient Israelites. The Israelite-Samaritans never left the land of Israel and did not wander to

Viiew of the sacred precinct on Mount Gerizim, looking west. Photo from:The New Encyclopedia of Archaeological Excavations in the Holy Land: Vol. 5, p. 1744.

other places. In the 127 generations since Joshua entered the land, they adhered to the God of Israel, his prophet Moses, the Torah of Moses and the place chosen by God – Mount Gerizim, as is clearly written in the Book of Deuteronomy at the end of chapter 11 and the beginning of chapter 12.

This, then, is their true identity: Children of Israel who preserve the true tradition of the people of Israel. The Israelite-Samaritans are the unique continuation of the ancient people of Israel.

We have now seen who the Israelite-Samaritans are. Which brings us to the question what are the Israelite-Samaritans?

The Israelite-Samaritans are a small community, part of the people of Israel, existing despite all the confrontations and controversies characteristic of the Middle East. Because they have a script, language and tradition thousands of years old which distinguishes them from all other national groups in the world, they have every right to regard themselves as a particular people.

In March 2017 they numbered 800 souls; this number gives hope for the future, seeing that it is five times as large as it was three generations ago, and the majority of them are children and youngsters.

The Samaritans are a small, special people that seeks peace. It is a people that does not stand at one end of the bridge to peace, or at the other end. The Israelite-Samaritans are a bridge, a bridge to peace with a national lifestyle of peaceful coexistence with all elements and political entities in the Middle East. For that reason, because they are a model of living together with all elements and are well-disposed to all that come and visit their neighborhoods, the Israelite-Samaritans are very welcome guests in the homes of prime minister Binyamin Netanyahu in Jerusalem, the president of the Palestinian Authority Mahmoud Abbas in Ramallah and King Abdullah in Amman, in the British parliament and Foreign Office in London, in the White House and the office of the American Secretary of State in Washington and in the offices of the European Union in Brussels.

An observer will see that people from all parts of the world come to see the Passover sacrifice, and in this way the prophecy is fulfilled that the peoples will come together in peace on the mountain-top, which is not in Jerusalem but in the chosen place, Mount Gerizim. He will see the Palestinian mayors of Nablus and Palestinian and Israeli officers sitting together in an atmosphere of peace. This is the modest contribution of the ancient Israelite-Samaritan people for the hoped-for peace in the whole region for the first time since the days of our Forefather Abraham.

The people of the holy Torah have a special history and an ancient and modern literature, special leaders, ancient poetry and music, a rich social and sporting life, an archaeological site of vast dimensions on Mount Gerizim which is evidence of their special material culture, an ethnic cuisine, one of the oldest in the world: all this, and more. They are a subject of great interest that draws hundreds of thousands of visitors every year to their centers.

5. The Samaritan Pentateuch

Holding up the Torah at Shavuot, on Mount Gerizim
Photo: Ori Orhof

The Israelite-Samaritans have consecrated only the five books of the Pentateuch. The Israelite-Samaritan version of the Pentateuch [SP] differs from the Jewish Masoretic Text [MT]. There are approximately 6,000 differences, most of them due to different spelling.

In the Hebrew University in Jerusalem, Dr. R. Weiss, the brilliant researcher of the relationship between the Septuagint Greek translation of the Pentateuch and the Samaritan Pentateuch, discovered that in 1,900 cases of the differences from the Masoretic text, the text of the Septuagint is identical with the Samaritan Pentateuch.

As we know that there are between 6,000 to 7,000 differences between the Samaritan Pentateuch and the Masoretic text, and approximately 50% of them are orthographic, it appears that the 1,900 differences are in the actual text and style of the writing. It follows that the Septuagint is much closer to the Samaritan Pentateuch than to the Masoretic text.

This leads us to the conclusion that the translators of the Septuagint had before them texts that were closer to the Samaritan Pentateuch, such as those found in Qumran cave 4, known as "proto-Samaritan" texts, written in the same ancient Hebrew script by Jewish writers. These Qumran texts and the earlier texts in the hands of the translators of the Septuagint are the earliest texts of the Pentateuch known today. Thus, the Samaritan Pentateuch presents the reader with the earliest known version. Hence, the Masoretic text is a version that elaborated in a later period – the second part of the Second Temple period.

The Caves at Qumran & Plan of the Site

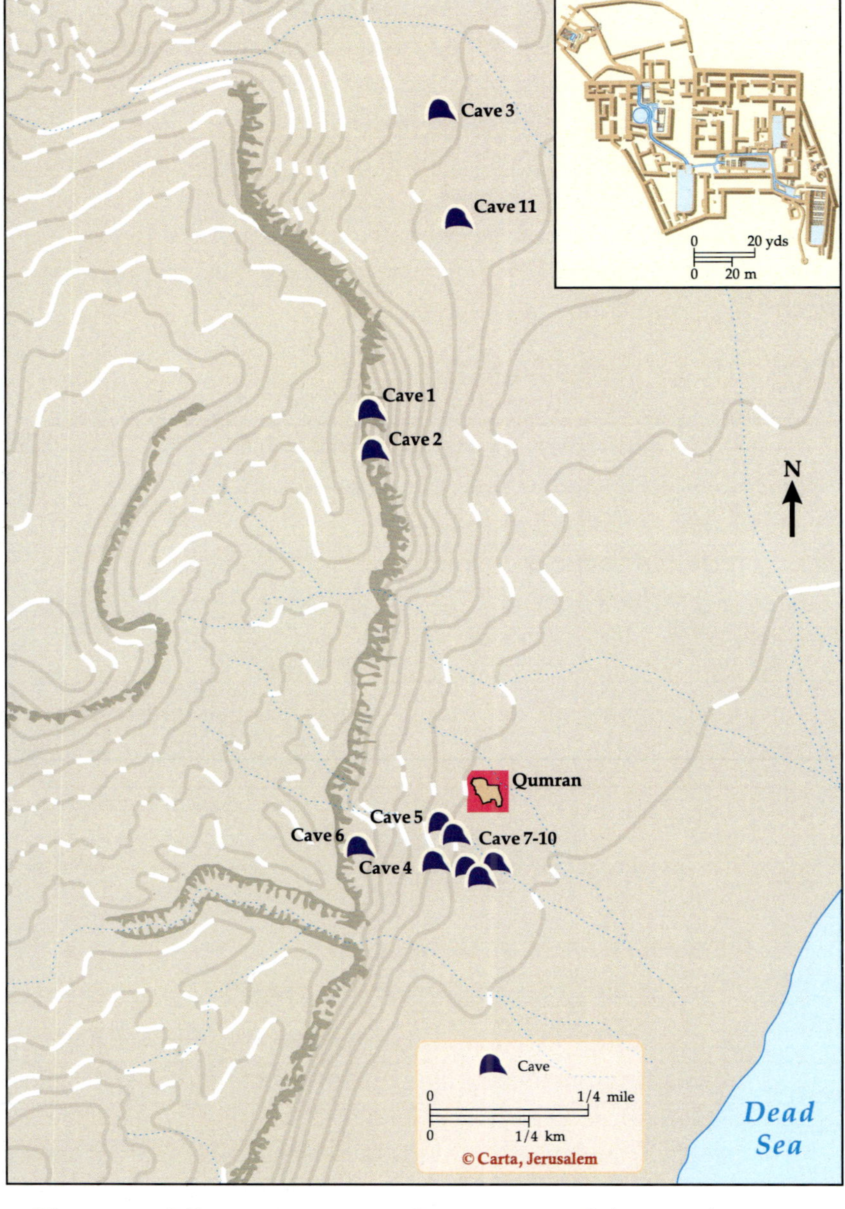

The main differences concern the question of the site the Almighty chose as His dwelling, to put His name there. In twenty-two verses of the Samaritan version of the Book of Deuteronomy, it is written: "In the place that the Almighty HAS CHOSEN," and in the Jewish Masoretic version the parallel verse reads: "In the place that the Almighty WILL CHOOSE."

In July 2008, the Princeton Theological Seminary researcher, Prof. James Charlesworth, placed on the internet an unknown fragment containing Deuteronomy 27:4-6, said to be taken from cave 4 in Qumran, giving the commandment to build an altar to the Almighty "In Mount Gerizim," spelled in one word of seven letters in Hebrew: בהרגרזים. This is an incredible discovery that should be examined carefully.

It is suggested that the spelling of the name of Mount Gerizim in one word and the commandment to build an altar to the Almighty upon it should no longer be seen as Samaritan or Jewish but as an ancient Israelite text dating from before the split between the Jews and Samaritans after the time of Alexander the Great, at the end of the fourth century BCE.

A page from the great Isaiah Scroll, Qumran
Carta, Jerusalem

The Israelite-Samaritans claim that the place had already been chosen at the time of the Pentateuch, which explains the use of the past tense - HAS CHOSEN, and this was Mount Gerizim, the only mountain in the Land of Israel that is designated in the Pentateuch for the offering of blessings (*Deuteronomy 11:29 and 27:12*), and that is where Abraham and Jacob built altars. As against them, the Jews claim that the place was chosen in the time of the Davidic and Solomonic kingdom (1000-930 BCE) and thus the use of the future tense, WILL CHOOSE, refers to the Temple Mount in Jerusalem.

There are several passages in the two versions of the Pentateuch (the Samaritan and the Masoretic) in which a text is written in one version and missing in the other. In the Ten Commandments (*Exodus 20:1-14, Deuteronomy 5:6-18*), the tenth commandment in the Samaritan version is the commandment to build an altar on Mount Gerizim. This commandment is missing in the Jewish Masoretic text.

However, in order to make the number of commandments up to ten the Jews made the opening words, the introduction: "I am Yhwh your God" the first commandment, although these words are not a commandment but an introduction. The second commandment in the Jewish Masoretic text is the first commandment in the Samaritan Pentateuch: "You shall have no other gods..."

Moreover, in chapters Deuteronomy 11 and 12, the commandment to offer the blessing on Mount Gerizim is given at the end of chapter 11, naming the location, and right after this, in chapter 12, the commandment is given to destroy all other places of worship, and worship only in the place chosen. As the reader of the chapter knows beyond any doubt that the sanctification of the Temple Mount in Jerusalem took place at a later period under King David and his son Solomon, it is clear that the intention of these chapters in Deuteronomy 11 and 12 is that the chosen place is Mount Gerizim.

In 2013, after ten years of work, the first English translation of the Samaritan Pentateuch (published by Eerdmans, Grand Rapids, Michigan) was completed. It gives in parallel columns the translation of the Samaritan text opposite a translation of the Jewish text, with an emphasis on the differences between the two versions given in bold capital letters.

In a third column, on the left, are notes expounding the views of the Samaritan Sages on the main differences between the two versions. The editor and translator of this edition is Benyamim Tsedaka, head of A.B. – Institute of Samaritan Studies, Holon, Israel (co-ed. Sharon Sullivan).

The four signs of identification

To be a member of the Israelite-Samaritan people one must adhere to the four signs of identification:

1. Perpetual residence in the Holy Land.
2. Obligatory participation in the Sacrifice on Mount Gerizim at Passover.
3. Celebration of the Sabbath as written in the Torah.
4. Adherence to the laws of purity and impurity as prescribed in the Torah.

6. Special Features of the Samaritans

Throughout the whole of history, the Samaritans never lost their unique status and image as a people. They have their own form of writing, the ancient Hebrew script; they speak their own language, the ancient Hebrew dialect spoken by Jews until the beginning of the first millennium CE; and they are raised in accordance with a unique, millennia-old historical tradition, dating back to the return of the people of Israel to its homeland under Joshua.

The four principles of faith

The Samaritans are guided by four principles of faith:

1. One God, who is the God of Israel;
2. One prophet, Moses son of Amram;
3. One holy book, the Pentateuch: the Torah handed down by Moses;
4. One holy place, Mount Gerizim.

To these is added belief in the Taheb, son of Joseph, the "Prophet like Moses" who will appear on the Day of Wrath and Judgement in the latter times.

7. Samaritan Prayers

Israelite-Samaritan prayer derived in the beginning from the written Torah and from the four great principles of belief in the One God, in His prophet Moses, in His holy Torah and in His sole sacred site, Mount Gerizim. Later, other principles were added like belief in the End of Days, punishment and reward, and the sanctity of observance of the Sabbath and the Holy Days.

Prayers and sacrifices in ancient times

In the earliest times, the second and first millennia BCE, prayer was derived solely from the written Torah and from the ancient poems including such as the "Song of the Sea," the "Song of Balaam" and the poem "Ha'azinu." For most of this period, the prayers accompanied the sacrifices which the priests offered on the altar of the tabernacle of Moses where they sacrificed and burned incense in God's presence.

When the sacrifices were made on Mount Gerizim with the disappearance of the tabernacle, they continued to pray as their predecessors and Moses prayed before God. They read the Torah every day of their lives and especially on the Sabbath, as on weekdays they were obliged to make a living. They read the Torah in the original Hebrew, and in Greek translation when they lived outside Israel. (Sections of the Greek translation of the Torah according to the Israelite-Samaritan rite are to be found today in the library of the University of Essen in Germany.)

The Passover sacrifice

[An example of the development of prayer]

In the period of Hellenistic rule, the great priestly house descended from Pinhas, the supreme institution of the Israelite-Samaritan people after its final split with the Israelite Jewish people in the late 4th century BCE, decreed that prayers would finally replace the sacrifices of the Torah except in the case of the Passover sacrifice, which was not included in the sacrifices made in the tabernacle but was made by the entire people of Israel. The Passover sacrifice is in fact the most characteristic example of the transitional stage from sacrifice to prayer, the sacrificing being accompanied by prayers written by Samaritan *paytanim* (liturgical poets).

In the first stage, passages of the Torah were simply read relating the exodus from Egypt, the "Song of the Sea," the Jethro episode, and the passage from "these were the journeys" to "keep the month of Aviv." In the second stage, at the beginning of the first millennium CE, they began to add the *piyyutim* (liturgical poems) of the first celebrated sage of the Israelite-Samaritans, Amram ben Sarad, who wrote in Aramaic.

At the Passover sacrifice, they sang his works "Merciful God, deliver us in thy mercy," and "Blessed is the house of Jacob and the source which derived from it," and the poem ascribed to his son Marqeh. In the second millennium, there were added the poem of Rabban Pinhas Ben Yosef ben Azi, which was

Pre-dawn pilgrimage on Mount Gerizim
Photo: Ori Orhof

later transferred to the service of the Day of Atonement, and the poem of the son of High Priest Eleazar ben Pinhas, "the honoured God is One, there is no other," sometimes sung in place of the later poem composed by the High Priest Amram ben Shalma (1809-1874), and was added to the service of the Passover sacrifice only in the nineteen-twenties.

The first stage

If there were *piyyutim* in Greek, which was the international language in the Hellenic period, they have not survived till now. Only one fragment survives from the end of the circumcision ceremony and some obscure words in a 14th-century poem sung at the end of the Sabbath prayers on the feast of Tabernacles.

In the introduction to his work "The Book of Days," the Damascus historian Abi Haftah ben Av-Hisda Hadanfi said that he omitted names and expressions in Greek when he copied from historical sources because they would not be understood by the people of his generation. It seems that Greek was used in ceremonies outside the synagogue but was not permitted within it.

This author has no doubt that *piyyutim* were written in Hebrew at that period which have not survived, for according to the "Book of Days" the meter of this poetry was fixed by the High Priests in the Hellenistic period.

The second stage

In the second stage of the development of prayer at the beginning of the first millennium CE, prayer developed through the creation of a new element which did not exist previously: the collection of passages from the Torah in accordance with religious events. This was called *ketef* (plucking). Passages were "plucked" from the Torah relating to the Sabbath, followed by "pluckings" for the Holy days and festivals, "pluckings" for each of the seven stations of pilgrimage, "pluckings" for the six Sabbaths on Shavu'ot, "pluckings" for every Rosh Hodesh, and so forth. The "plucking" is thus the first element we have of the full version of the Torah from the end of the first millennium BCE. From a perusal of early manuscripts of prayers we see that in places where there were large concentrations of Samaritans - Nablus, Damascus, Cairo, Gaza and Ashkelon – there were special pluckings of the Torah. Some early pluckings from Damascus and Nablus have survived till today.

The third stage

In the first centuries CE, Aramaic replaced Greek as the universal language, and by a natural process daily speech influenced Samaritan prayer at that period. From the third to the fifth centuries CE, we have a special collection of *piyyutim* by the threesome Amram, his son Marqah and his grandson Nana, and the marvellous work, the only one that remains from the sage Yehoshua Ben Barak Ben Eden, "The Merciful God Will Reign For Ever." Through a misunderstanding of his name, this *piyyut* was called "the prayer of Joshua."

In this period, Israelite-Samaritan prayer was said in the source language, Hebrew, combined with passages from *piyyutim* and prayers in a Samaritan form of Aramaic. Most of the people spoke Aramaic, and did not speak Hebrew. Thus, a family of priests of the house of Itamar had the task of setting the order of prayers in the synagogue and translating the Hebrew of the prayers into Aramaic for the benefit of the congregants. At the end of the period, the great *piyyutim* mentioned above were added to the liturgy of the Samaritan synagogue and were an outstanding feature of the Samaritan cult in its golden age under Byzantine rule. It was at this period, under Roman and Byzantine rule, that a translation was made of the Torah into Samaritan Aramaic.

The inclusion of Aramaic

The order of prayer crystallized in the Byzantine period still continued to develop when the Arabs succeeded the Byzantines in ruling the land of Israel and neighboring countries where there were concentrations of Samaritans. But neither Latin nor Arabic, which were international languages, or Greek before them, were incorporated in the liturgy of the synagogue. Arabic words were only used in ceremonies and events outside the synagogue on joyful or sad occasions in Samaritan life, or in commentaries, translations, books of history, and so on.

The liturgy of the synagogue was restricted to only two languages: the language of the Torah and the Aramaic language, which was commonly spoken by the Samaritans in daily life until the tenth century CE. Samaritans who knew Greek through their involvement in international trade still wrote *piyyutim* of a high literary level in Aramaic.

The exalted style of the *piyyutim* of the Aldustan family in the sixth century CE, facilitated their insertion into the liturgy of the synagogue, and the same applied to those of Tabia Ibn Darta in the eighth century CE, when Aramaic, and among part of the people, Greek, was still commonly spoken by Samaritans.

At the beginning of the second millennium CE, in the eleventh and twelfth centuries, more Aramaic works were added to the liturgy. The first centuries of the second millennium CE were also a fruitful period for Samaritan works in Arabic. There was a translation of the Torah into Arabic, commentaries on the Torah in that language, and works dealing with the calendar, etc.

Samaritans at prayer
Photo: Ori Orhof

Raising the Torah Scroll in prayer
Photo: Ori Orhof

The fourth stage

The Fourth stage in the development of Samaritan prayer took place during the fourteenth century under the direction of several consecutive High Priests. There were many works in Aramaic and "Samaritan Hebrew" – a mixture of Hebrew and Aramaic – and the order of prayers came into being which is still used today: a combination of "pluckings" and verses from the Torah, *piyyutim* from the early sages and *piyyutim* from that period.

The "dedication of the soul"

The fourteenth-century sages also created the opening formula of every prayer-service called "the dedication of the soul," which is in a mixture of Aramaic and Hebrew. In the dedication, one bows in the direction of Mount Gerizim with one's head resting on the palms of one's hands and prays in a whisper, and then one stands up and continues the prayer.

There is a shortened version for weekdays and Sabbath eve. The mixed language of the "dedication of the soul" shows that it was written in the time when "Samaritan Hebrew" was used, the second millennium CE.

The order of prayer in our time

The compilers of prayer-books quite naturally added on to the works of their contemporaries, and so it continued, generation after generation. But the basis of the service in synagogues today was essentially laid by the sages of the fourteenth century.

For hundreds of years, until the eighteenth century, the most pious members of the congregation would sit in the synagogue from Sabbath eve or the eve of festivals until the end of the Sabbath or the festival, and the family would bring them their food in the synagogue. Later, from the nineteenth century until today, the congregation would come to the synagogue at fixed hours.

Summary

First stage, to the end of the first millennium BCE: simply reading of the Torah.

Second stage, in the first centuries of the 1st millennium CE, "pluckings" were added.

Third stage, in the 4th and 5th centuries CE, the first liturgical poems in Aramaic were added.

Fourth stage, in the 14th century CE the fixed prayer service was created which is still used.

8. Calculation of the Calendar

The Jewish and Samaritan calculations of the calendar are very similar. The differences between the two systems stem from the opening year of each calculation.

The Jewish calculation starts from the first year of the creation according to the Jewish counting, but the Samaritan calendar starts from the first year of entering Israel with Joshua Bin-Nun, to the Samaritan Counting and hence the leap years in both calendars are not parallel.

Thus, the Samaritan festivals sometimes take place 30 days after the same Jewish ones. Both festivals generally take place on the same days, but the Samaritans very often celebrate one or two days before the Jews because in certain years when the festival falls close to the Sabbath, the Jews add one day to their month of Kislev.

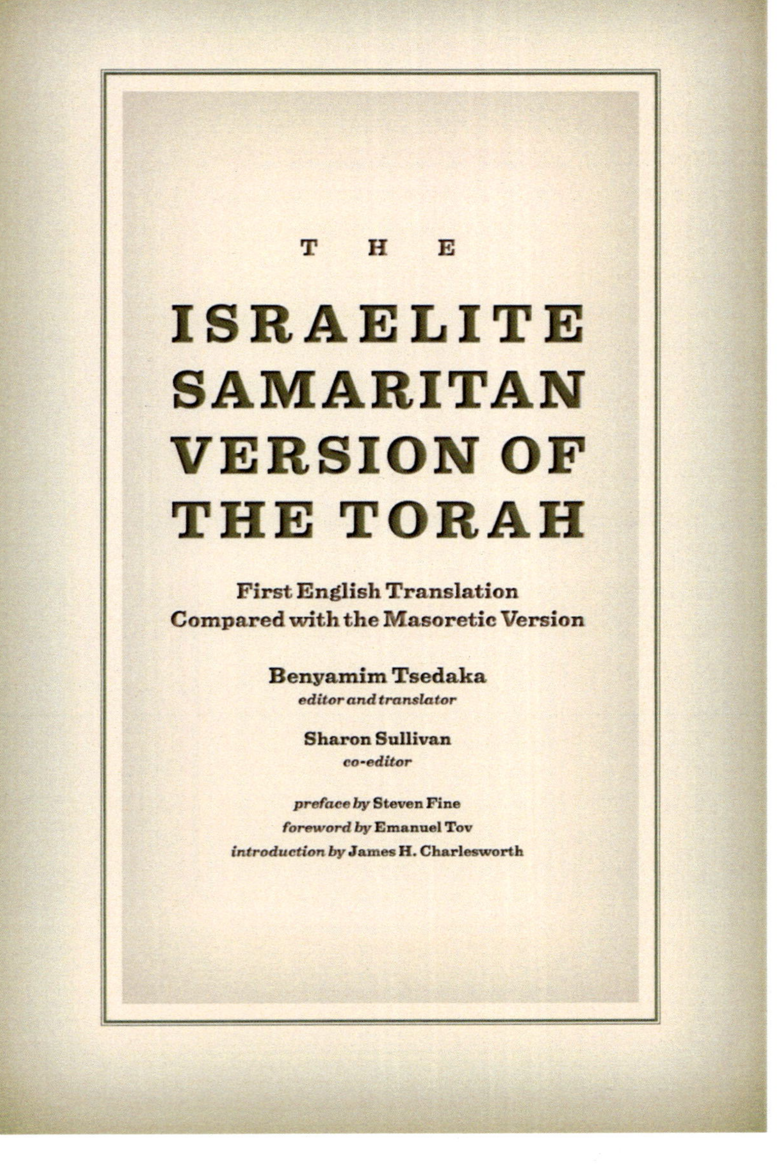

The front cover of the first English translation of the Israelite-Samaritan Version of the Torah

9. Sabbaths and Holy Days. Sabbath Observance among the Israelite-Samaritans.

The Sabbath is the holiest of the seven days of the week. It lasts from sundown on Friday to sundown on Saturday. On the Sabbath the lives of the Samaritans are different from their lives during the week, and the preparation for it is, therefore, also different from other days. The same can be said of the festivals, for according to the tradition of the Torah, one acts in the same way on them as on the Sabbath.

With two differences: if the pilgrimage festivals, Passover, Weeks, and Tabernacles, occur on a weekday, the concession of travelling by vehicle is permitted for people outside the community for pilgrimage to the place chosen by the Almighty. The saving of life overrules the Sabbath, for life takes precedence over death in the Torah - "and you shall live by them." In cases of birth or mortal illness, everything must be done to bring a person to immediate medical treatment, even if it involves the use of a vehicle, forbidden on the Sabbath.

The Israelite-Samaritans honour the Sabbath and observe it punctiliously. On Friday afternoons the whole community and every family prepare for the Sabbath. Everyone in the house prepares for the Sabbath. The men take off their weekday clothes and put on a garment extending from the shoulders to the knees. It is made of thin white material in spring and summer, and wool in autumn and winter. The garment is fastened with a button and a buttonhole around the neck, and on the hips with a girdle made of the same material as the garment. And on both sides there are large pockets (mainly for handkerchiefs in autumn and winter, and for keys to the house for locking up on leaving for synagogue). In the front there is a tiny pocket which formerly contained a watch. Today it is replaced by a wristwatch, but the pocket remains.

Preparations for the Sabbath

The mother of the house and her daughters work at the final preparations for the Sabbath. In the case of a young couple who do not yet have children, the husband helps the wife with the preparations. If she is in her monthly menstrual period, the husband makes the preparations for the Sabbath. Hot water is kept in large thermos flasks. The lights are kept on from sabbath eve until the end of the Sabbath in the kitchen and in the main room of the house in which they sit down to meals and read the portion of the week. The practice of having the light on is chiefly in order to prevent situations of emergency and so to observe the commandment "not to set up an obstacle before the blind," for in total darkness everyone is as though blind.

Before the start of the Sabbath, they disconnect all electrical appliances in the house and shut the radio and television, computers and cell phones. For twenty-four hours, the Sabbath is devoted to the assembled family. One does not cook, one does not smoke, and one does not travel on the Sabbath. The special Sabbath costume restricts the members of the community to the confines of their neighborhood. The refrigerator is disconnected, and in the freezer iced water is kept which preserves the coldness of the refrigerator until the end of the Sabbath. A Sabbath clock or the use of electrical appliances on the Sabbath is not permitted. All this is considered a transgression of the commandment, "You shall not make a fire in your dwelling places on the Sabbath."

There is a controversy in the community about whether the use of an air-conditioner in the very hot summer days is permitted. Some use an air-conditioner, but most of the community on Mount Gerizim and in Holon do not. The High Priests have not made a decision on the matter and continue to look for a solution that will ease the situation of the congregation. One of the High Priests decreed that when there is a severe heat wave, morning and afternoon prayers can be read together. This matter is left to the discretion of the priest who leads the services. The women, still wearing their weekday clothes, prepare the Sabbath meals.

Preparations for the meal on Sabbath eve

The usual foods on the table on Sabbath eve are: Stuffed chicken with rice and spices. Vine-leaves or celery stuffed with rice and small pieces of chicken with fresh tomato sauce. Pieces of potato roasted in the oven with chicken and spices. This is called *tashtush*.

There are also additions:

* Bean soup or vegetable soup with rice and chicken, salt and lemon.

* A vegetable salad with tomatoes, cucumbers, radishes and lettuce cut up in small pieces, salt, olive oil, lemon and spices.

* The hot food is placed in dishes which are covered with a piece of fabric until worshippers come home from synagogue.

Group of Samaritans. From a photograph taken in 1861 by the Palestine Exploration Fund
From: The Jewish Encyclopedia, published between 1901 and 1906
Via Wikimedia Commons

* When the Sabbath begins, the women put on their best clothes. The women can wear trousers or slacks only on weekdays, not on the Sabbath.

The Israelite-Samaritan synagogue

The father and his sons dressed in the special garment go to the synagogue about an hour before sundown. At the entrance to the synagogue they take off their shoes and wear socks, or go barefoot in summer. They leave their shoes on shelves or on the floor of the small entrance hall in order to fulfil the commandment, "Put off your shoes from your feet."

The floor of the main synagogue is covered by a thick wall-to-wall carpet, suited to sitting cross-legged in the oriental style or standing up. Very old people and the disabled sit on small chairs. There are bound Pentateuchs and prayer books on small benches or shelves along the walls.

In the front of the synagogue there is an altar divided into two parts. In one part, at the back, sit the cantor and the High Priest. The front part is separated from the back part by a curtain, behind which there is the Holy Ark in which Scrolls of the Law are placed in metal cases. The cases and scrolls are taken out during morning and afternoon prayers to bless the congregation.

The members of the congregation usually sit in their habitual places in the synagogue. All are present. Only illness excuses a man from attending synagogue, and then he prays alone. Each person knows his place. Guests from outside the congregation sit at the back of the hall. Those cleansed from some uncleanliness before the Sabbath sit along the back wall of the synagogue. This is not considered a disgrace as it happens to everyone.

Women do not take part in the prayers. They come to the synagogue on the Day of Atonement and sit at the back of the hall. On the Sabbaths of the festivals, during morning prayers, they come to the synagogue for an hour, receive a blessing from the High Priest, and go home. Women having their period do not come to the synagogue and do not participate in the Passover Sacrifice and the pilgrimages.

Sitting on the plush carpet at the service in the synagogue.
Photo: Ori Orhof

The seven prayers on the Sabbath

Seven prayers are said on the Sabbath:

* Two are said on Sabbath eve.
* Two are said on Sabbath morning.
* Two are said in the afternoon.
* One at the end of the Sabbath.

The prayers on Sabbath eve

In the first prayer-service, all passages in the Torah which mention the Sabbath are read. The second prayer-service contains *piyyutim* and prayers. These two consecutive services begin about an hour before sunset and end when the sun goes down.

During prayers, people stand or sit in accordance with the order decided by the High Priest. Most of the prayers are recited by heart, and children read them from prayer books until they also know them by heart. When the congregants have to bend down, they go down on their knees and the head touches the carpet resting on the palms of the hands clasped together on

Bi-Lingual Pentateuch
Right: Hebrew, and Left: Arabic translation, both written in ancient Hebrew.
Cambridge University Library MS. Add. 714.
Source: Plate XI. The S.S. Teacher's Edition: The Holy Bible. New York: Henry Frowde, Publisher to the University of Oxford, 1896.
Via Wikimedia Commons

the carpet. When they simply bend over, they bow according to the order of prayers, inclining the upper part of the body from the hips upwards for a few seconds.

Most of the prayers are said aloud or sung by the whole congregation. The cantor has a brief role in the order of prayers. At the end of the prayers, the cantor mentions the Sabbath and the congregation replies "amen" a number of times. After that, they bend down and conclude the prayers.

After that, they stand, and the cantor leaves the congregation with the blessing, "May you have many good Sabbaths," and they reply in the same way. They all leave by the same exit. No sight is more unruly than that of the congregation leaving the synagogue and streaming right and left on their way to their homes.

Prayers, First of the Seventh Month, in the synagogue
Photo: Ori Orhof

At home, they sit at the Sabbath table, sing Sabbath songs and bless the wine. The women of the house take the coverings off the dishes and serve.

They eat in tranquillity. Sabbath is the opportunity for the whole family to come together: parents with children and the families of the sons and daughters. These arrive after the meal, sit for an hour or so, and are served tea and cakes prepared for the Sabbath. They talk about everything under the sun. At ten o'clock in the evening, the last ones go home to sleep in order to wake up for morning prayers.

The prayers on Sabbath morning

For morning prayers in the synagogue, the congregants wear white cotton prayer-shawls over their garments. The prayer-shawl extends from the shoulders to the soles of the feet. On the left and right there are openings to the pockets of the garment. On its upper right-hand side there are twenty-two buttons made of the same material as the prayer-shawl and on the left-hand side there are twenty-two buttonholes.

This corresponds to the number of letters of the alphabet in which the Torah is written. In the Hebrew-Samaritan script there are no final letters, as in ancient times. These are the *tsitsit*, the "specially knotted ritual fringes, or tassels" in the Israelite-Samaritan tradition.

On weekdays, the Israelite-Samaritans do not put on phylacteries as in rabbinic Judaism, but see phylacteries as reminders to remember God's commandments.

The cantor carrying the Torah-Scroll and unrolling it before the congregation wears, over his white prayer-shawl, a blue and white silk prayer-shawl, or a green and white one, with tassels, during the short time that he carries the case with the Torah-Scroll. When he puts the scroll back in the ark he folds up the silk prayer-shawl and leaves it there.

The men wear the prayer-shawl over their garments and go to synagogue. Prayers begin at 3.30 a.m. and end at six in the morning. The prayers include passages from the Torah and *piyyutim* [hymns]. This is the end of the first prayer-service.

The second morning prayer-service is the reading of the weekly portion. The congregants leave the synagogue and split up into small groups of ten to fifteen people and go to the home of the senior member of the group. There, they sit on a carpet along the walls of the large main room of the house and begin to chant the portion of the week. Men, children, boys and girls are all allowed to participate in the reading.

The portion is divided into sections and each of the participants chants a section to a slow melody. If there are more sections than participants, each person reads a second one rapidly.

At the end of the portion, the master of the house serves cups of tea, cakes and various pastries. They engage in noisy, lively conversation, and then each one goes home to eat breakfast. The morning hours until midday prayers are devoted to rest and sleep. The breakfast includes many kinds of tasty salads. It is recommended to prepare them according to the cookbook, *The Wonders of Israelite-Samaritan Cuisine* by the sisters Batia Tsedaka and Zippora Sassoni, published by the A.B. Institute of Samaritan Studies, Holon, 2011.

The ingredients for the salads are already in the refrigerator on Friday. Herbs and olive oil are added. There are light beverages, and some people drink wine, but not to the point of intoxication. The salads generally satisfy people for the whole day until the conclusion of the Sabbath. The women, after they have prepared breakfast, put on attractive dresses and blouses which display their beauty and go and visit their neighbors, or their neighbors visit them.

Midday prayers on the Sabbath

At midday, or at 1.00 p.m. in summer, they go to synagogue for two midday prayer services. The first service consists of sections of the Torah and *piyyutim*. The second service consists of *piyyutim* and a quick reading of the weekly portion. This is read alternately by those sitting on the right side of the hall of the synagogue and those sitting on the left side. Those on the right read a section and those on the left read the next one, and so on until the end of the portion They end with a short *piyyut* and go home. The cantor leaves the congregation, making a blessing, and the congregation responds in the same words. They take off their prayer-shawl and put it on a hanger. A light meal is waiting at home (a cold dessert in winter, a watermelon with home-made white cheese in summer).

From midday Sabbath until the evening

The time from midday to late afternoon on the Sabbath is used for visits to friends. If someone is hospitalized and sent home for the Sabbath, everyone visits him or her and asks after their welfare. If there was a celebration or loss during the week, they visit the family.

The afternoon is also used to gather children and adolescents for a reading of passages from the Torah, including the portion for the following week. This is done in order to teach children and young people to read the Torah without mistakes. Some learn *piyyyutim* from professional cantors that would be chanted in the synagogue in the near future on Holy Days, Sabbaths and festivals close to the time of learning.

Prayers for the end of the Sabbath

The prayers for the conclusion of the Sabbath begin about half an hour before sundown and end when the sun sets. The congregants pray in garments without prayer-shawls unless prayers for Rosh Hodesh are said at the end of the Sabbath, in which case prayer-shawls are worn. A central part of the service is an ancient *piyyut* on leaving the Sabbath. The prayers end with a final *piyyut*. The priest leaves the congregation with the blessing "Peace be unto you," and the congregants respond in the same way.

They go home after prayers and together sing a hymn of praise to Moses. The master of the house serves coffee in small cups. A new week begins. They take off their garments, fold them, put them in a cupboard and put on weekday clothes.

On Sabbaths during the festivals, or if a festival falls on a Sabbath, morning prayers are especially long. They begin at two in the morning and end at about nine in the morning. There are no midday prayers and the portion of the week is not read. On the Day of Atonement, prayers last for about twenty-five hours, from evening to evening, non-stop. If there is a circumcision on the Sabbath, prayers stop during the time of the ceremony, and then they return to the synagogue for the continuation of the prayers.

Children in the synagogue.
Photo: Ori Orhof

10. The Seven Samaritan Festivals

The 21 days of the first month. The first Rosh Hodesh (New Moon)

People gather in the synagogues and mark the Hebrew New Year with a special prayer service. At the end of the service they make the blessing, "May you have peace throughout the year," and at home there is a festive meal. That evening is the start of the fourteen days of watching.

The fourteen days of Keeping

These are the days of observing the month of Aviv and of guarding the sheep, from the tenth of the month to the paschal Sacrifice. In the first month, there are special prayers in the evening and morning.

The first Sabbath of the first month

On this Sabbath, the miracle of the plague of locusts is recalled in a prayer of joy at the approach of Passover. Two *piyyutim* are chanted by one of the congregants at morning and midday prayers on the splendor of the month of Aviv. After morning and midday prayers, the portion of the week is read.

The second Sabbath of the first month

On this Sabbath, the miracle of the plague of darkness is recalled in a prayer of joy at the approach of Passover. Two *piyyutim* are chanted by one of the congregants at morning and midday prayers on the splendor of the paschal Sacrifice. After morning and midday prayers, the portion of the week is read.

The tenth day of the first month

On the ten first days of the month, the whole family goes out to the flock of sheep near Kiryat Luza and buys from its owner a one year-old unblemished lamb. Each person who acquires a lamb keeps him in the yard of his home, feeds him and protects him from injury. In the fourteen days of watching, the whole family cleans the house, paints it up to make it look presentable, removes the leavened bread and puts it out of sight in a place sealed off until the end of the days of *matzot* (unleavened bread). (People always purchase extra sheep for the days of *matzot* in case, in the time of the Sacrifice, one of the sheep would be found unsuitable for sacrifice, if the slaughtering is not in order, or if there is some defect.)

There is a Samaritan legend that the sheep strive between themselves to be the one to be sacrificed. This is all very well for those who make the sacrifice, but not so pleasant for the sheep!

The day of the Sacrifice – the fourteenth day of the first month

The High Priest and his entourage come to the place of sacrifice at the heart of Kiryat Luza where there is an earthen altar and six ovens dug into the earth, used for roasting the sacrifice. Time is short, for a fire can be lit in the ovens and on the altar only at the end of the Sabbath, which is the time for slaughtering the sheep for the paschal sacrifice.

Prayers start about half an hour before the slaughtering begins. The High Priest and the other priests and the notables in the congregation, all dressed in white garments and prayer-shawls, go up to the front of the place of sacrifice. The eastern wall is adorned with verses from the Torah connected with the exodus from Egypt and the Passover. At the central point of the front area stands a high moveable pulpit which the High Priest ascends at the end of the opening prayer of the sacrifice.

The prayers consist of an opening section and *piyyutim* chanted by the people to the left and right. Those on the right are notables wearing white garments and prayer-shawls, and those on the left are those who slaughter wearing the garments of the exodus from Egypt – trousers and a simple white cotton shirt, and the oldest among them have staffs in their hands, as if Moses were to come at any moment and call on them to follow him. On the right side of the area there are chairs for important visitors, and on the left side there are chairs for elderly Samaritans. Most of the notables stand and chant *piyyutim* (hymns).

The Israelite-Samaritan women come to the ceremony in their best clothes. Until then, they had helped their husbands and families in cleaning the house and baking the *matzot*. The *matzot* were mainly baked the previous evening, and a small number are baked on the day of the sacrifice. The flour for the *matzot* is ground and cleaned about two months before the Passover, and is stored until the *matzot* are baked on the previous day. Great care is taken to ensure that the dough is not leavened. The round, flat *matzot* contain salt, an essential part of the sacrifice.

About two hours before the sacrifice, one of the priests comes to supervise the lighting of the six ovens with wood. The ovens are in operation for the next six hours. Towards the time of the sacrifice, the wood on the altar is set alight to burn up all parts of the animals not allowed to be eaten. The altar is made of earth, a kind of tunnel dug out of the earth, sufficiently long enough to contain all the sheep destined for sacrifice. At the head of the channel, a round hole is dug on which an iron net with wood underneath is placed. On the altar, the parts of the animals not eaten are burned as is specified in the Book of Leviticus. On the left-hand side of the area of the sacrifice, the six ovens are operated by six members of the congregation who feed the flames until the stones of the oven are whitened by the intense heat of the fire.

The Sacrifice

The chanting stops: the great moment has come. The High Priest ascends the pulpit and begins to read the portion of the exodus from Egypt (*Exodus, chapter 12*): "And God spoke to Moses and Aaron in the land of Egypt, saying..." The High Priest reads in a loud and clear voice. The notables follow his reading with grunts and with mounting interest. While he reads, the group of those who make the sacrifice, who are generally young, take hold of the sheep and bind them with their hands on both sides of the channel of the altar, and they and the slaughterers wait tensely for the words permitting the slaughter to begin.

The High Priest continues to read in a loud voice: "And ye shall have a watch until the fourteenth day of this month," and then continues loudly and with greater emphasis: "And you shall slaughter it." The excitement of the Israelite-Samaritan crowd erupts ecstatically. The nimble slaughterers go from sheep to sheep and slaughter them. The sacrificers cry loudly a number of times, "The Almighty is One!"

To the sacrifice ceremony
Photo: Ori Orhof

The High Priest ends his reading of the passage. The notables come up to him, kiss his right hand, and wish him a year of prosperity, and he gives each one his blessing and a warm smile. The notables embrace and bless each other, and the sacrificers do likewise. No other time is as beautiful as this except for the end of the Day of Atonement.

The time comes for the slaughterers to conclude the work of preparing the slaughtered sheep for roasting. Each slaughterer takes charge of his family's sheep. There are sufficient slaughterers, and each year they are joined by new ones. The slaughterer flays the sheep and sends it to be roasted in the heated ovens, and he removes the inedible parts, including the thigh muscle, and youths take them to the altar to be burnt. He removes the edible inner parts such as the liver, heart and lungs, washes them thoroughly and replaces them inside the sheep which has been washed out. He severs its front right leg and sends it to the place where all the right legs are deposited. They are distributed amongst the priests' families.

After another thorough washing, a three-meter long wooden spit is inserted into each sheep through the throat. The sheep is bound to the spit. It is well salted inside and out, and is placed with the spit on the wall in front of the ovens for about two hours until all the blood that remains in it has drained off.

During the preparation of the sheep for roasting, the other sacrificers gather around the slaughterers and the sheep, and joyfully and in a loud voice read the passages in the Bible on the exodus from Egypt interspersed with passages from a *piyyut* on the same subject.

The sacrificers dip their finger in the blood of the slaughtered sheep and smear a drop on the forehead of their firstborn sons. A priest goes by with a basket full of bitter herbs, of which there are masses on Mount Gerizim, combined with pieces of matzah. All the sacrificers take some matzah and bitter herbs and eat them as a symbol of the hasty exodus from Egypt when the Israelites prepared the sacrifice.

The sacrifice ceremony
Photo: Ori Orhof

About two and a half hours after the beginning of the slaughter, the sacrificers gather around the ovens. Each of the strong young men holds a spit in his hands, and after a short prayer, at an agreed sign from the priest organizing the sacrifice, they insert the spits in the ovens. Fifty years ago, the small community that existed at that time used only one oven, but now there are six or seven.

Next to each oven there are rectangular metal bowls heaped with dust. The dust is mixed with water until it becomes like a dough. Some of this "dough" of dark brown earth is used to stop up the opening of the pipe. After the insertion of the spits, a heavy iron net is placed on their ends to steady them.

A piece of wet jute is immediately

placed on the net, and some of the "dough" from the rectangular metal containers is put on it. The dough of wet brown earth is spread on the fabric until the openings are sealed and there is complete closure of the mouth of the oven. Only the ends of the long spits protrude from the material. The fire of the oven is extinguished for lack of oxygen, and what remains in the oven is the tremendous heat given off by the rectangular stones of the oven and the burning wood at the bottom. The sheep are roasted in this heat for two whole hours.

In the two hours when the sheep are being roasted, the sacrificers gather under the large awning which covers the place of sacrifice. They sit on lightweight chairs and chant *piyyutim* pertaining to the festival. The chanting is continuous. The older members of the group take a short break, take refreshments prepared for the festival, and tell the many visitors about the community and the ceremony of sacrifice.

Around midnight

Towards midnight, at the height of the sacrifice service which begins at dusk with the slaughtering, in the minutes before and after 11.30 p.m., on a sign from the priest responsible and a short prayer, spades clear away the ashes from the oven. The strong young men together lift the heavy netting and remove it from the oven.

Each sacrificer takes his spit with the sheep that is on it. Each sheep is wrapped in a light and supple metal net so that its inner parts will not fall to the bottom of the oven during the roasting.

The sheep are immediately taken from the spits to smooth white wooden bowls. The spits are then thrown into the oven to be burned.

Then the whole congregation gathers with the roasted sheep under the awning and they all chant a *piyyut*. The oldest priest present blesses the congregation at the end of it. Some of the sacrificers remain behind and eat the sacrifice hastily with *matzot* and bitter herbs, and most of them carry off the wooden bowls and sing the "Song of the Sea" on their way home.

In the large room at home or on a balcony, the smooth wooden bowl is placed on the floor. Men and women sit around the dish and eat. Each one holds a piece of matzah and bitter herbs and eats it with the sheep. The whole process is very quick, as the Israelites left Egypt in haste. After about twenty minutes, one of the young men takes the dish and the meat left on it to the altar to be burned.

Some young people supervise the burning and the others go home to rest before Passover prayers at five in the morning. The prayers touch off the Feast of Matzot which begins as soon as they end. Then they go home for a long rest until the following afternoon.

The seven days of the Feast of Matzot

The main item on the menu on these days is lamb and matzot.

Making Matzot, for the Feast of Matzot
Photo: Ori Orhof

Passover pilgrimage on Mount Gerizim
Photo: Ori Orhof

They are careful to eat what they have cooked and not to buy the meat. The drink is restricted to water, or water with lemon or pomegranate juice. Every two days *matzot* are baked for the following two days.

On the days of the festival, the families visit one another. On the morning of the sacrifice, many visit the graves of relatives and pray for their souls.

The Sabbath on the Feast of Matzot

There is a special Sabbath between the first day of the festival and the pilgrimage on the seventh day. There are special prayers with hymns and *piyyutim* about the exodus from Egypt. At the meal on the morning of the Sabbath there are special dishes for the occasion. This Sabbath is particularly joyful. The women wear their best clothes and at the end of the week visit their friends.

The first day: the beginning of the Counting of the Omer, the day after the Sabbath

The Counting of the Omer begins on the day after the Sabbath after the Passover sacrifice. It ends on Shavuot (the Feast of Weeks), the fiftieth day of the Counting of the Omer.

The seventh day of the Feast of Matzot, the day of the first pilgrimage

Three feasts in the year last seven days. The seven days of the Feast of Matzot are in Passover, and on all these days *matzot* are eaten. Shavuot lasts seven days, from the preceding Monday to the Sunday of the week in which the feast is observed. Succoth (The Feast of Tabernacles) lasts seven days, from the first day to the eve of Shemini Atzeret (the Eighth Day of Assembly).

On the eve of the Feast of Matzot there are special prayers. Very early in the morning, at 2.00 a.m., people gather in the great synagogue on Mount Gerizim, and at about 4.30 a.m., after prayers lasting two hours, they leave the synagogue and go up to the crest of the mountain. They all wear a special garment and a prayer-shawl.

They go up to the summit, a distance of about three hundred meters. When it is not on a Sabbath, the use of vehicles driven by non-Samaritans to take old people and the disabled is permitted.

The seven stations of the pilgrimage.

When they reach the summit, they stop next to the stones placed there by Joshua Bin Nun as the base of the first altar built by the people of Israel. Recently, a fragment was discovered at Qumran, near the Dead Sea, containing verses 4-6 of chapter seven of the Book of Deuteronomy in Aramaic, which speak of the laying of the stones of the altar on Mount Gerizim. (In the Masoretic version it is Mount Ebal.) It resembles the words of the tenth commandment in Exodus, chapter 20, and Deuteronomy, chapter 5, in the Samaritan Pentateuch. In the Jewish version there are nine commandments plus a fill-in. The pilgrims stand by the stones and read the relevant verse from Deuteronomy three times.

From there they go on to the second station on the mountain, the site of the altar of Adam and his son Seth, and there the priest declaims "Praise the Almighty" After that, they continue on their way, singing, to the third station — a flat rock in the center of the summit, where according to tradition Joshua erected the tabernacle. Here, facing the Hill of Eternity, they conclude the first part of the prayers. The priest blesses those present when they finish and gives a sign to begin the great journey to the summit with the "Song of the Sea."

The pilgrims join him joyously and begin to walk in exemplary order to the third station: the place where the ram appeared in the bush to Abraham, who sacrificed it in place of his son. There, while the priest unfurls a Torah-scroll, they blast five times on a shofar, saying, "God will provide, God will provide!."

The priest blesses the crowd once again.

Israelite-Samaritan Priests with ancient Torah scroll
Painted by Miriam Tsedaka

From there, the pilgrims proceed to the next station, "Isaac's altar," also called "Abraham's altar." Here the pilgrims gather around a rock shaped like an altar and read the story of the Akkedah (the Sacrifice of Isaac). This is based on an earlier tradition than the Jewish one, which made Jerusalem the site of the Akkedah.

The pilgrims go up to the rock and touch it, and wish each other good fortune. Then they join the others going to the next station. This is a few meters to the west of "Isaac's altar" and was the site of "Noah's altar." According to the tradition, when Noah left the ark he went to Mount Gerizim and built an altar. Here, the pilgrims recall Noah, the ark and the altar. Then they go on to the next station, the seventh, on their way back to the Hill of Eternity.

On the way to the Hill of Eternity, the pilgrims split up into two groups.

The pilgrims go up to the rock barefoot and sit or stand as the prayers require. The High Priest gives them seven blessings. Then there is another prayer. The pilgrims embrace one another and wish each other well. Then they go home. At home, there is a farewell meal with a return to leaven.

The pilgrimage also takes place on Shavuot and Succoth.

The seven days of the Feast of Shavuot, the Day of Assembly, the Night of Reading the Torah and the Day of the Revelation of Sinai

Between the Feast of Matzot and the Feast of Shavuot, the Israelite-Samaritans mark the seven stages the children of Israel passed through in the Sinai Desert on their way from the Red Sea to Mount Sinai in order to receive the Ten Commandments, the Torah and the *mitzvot*. The first station is that of the Red Sea, the second that of Marah, the third Ilim, the fourth the Desert of Zin where manna came down from heaven, the fifth Rephidim, where Moses took water out of the rock at Horeb, and the sixth, Joshua Bin Nun's war against Amalek.

On the forty-fourth day of the Counting of the Omer, there is the Day of Assembly, the day the children of Israel began to assemble for the revelation of Sinai. This is the first day

Shavuot pilgrimage
Photo: Ori Orhof

of the seven days of Shavuot. On that evening, there is the Night of the Reading of the Torah, the night on which they remember the historical event of the giving of the Torah on Mount Sinai which falls on the forty-sixth day of the Counting of the Omer.

On that evening, there is a special prayer-service, and at its conclusion, a festive meal. That night and the following day – the Day of the Revelation of Sinai – are working days. But, already, close to midnight, the Day of the Revelation of Sinai begins, with many *piyyutim* and a reading of the whole Torah. Families compete in offering drinks and special cakes prepared for the occasion. There is much joy. Those that have to go to work on that day are permitted to do so, but most people remain in the synagogue until the end of the day.

The forty-seventh and forty-eighth days of the Counting of the Omer are a time of rejoicing, and then one comes to the Sabbath, the forty-ninth day. There are especially long prayers on that Sabbath, and all the *piyyutim* chanted then are about the Revelation of Sinai. At the end of the day, eve of Shavuot prayers begin. On Shavuot, the second pilgrimage of the year takes place on the fiftieth day of the Counting of the Omer. The order of the pilgrimage is the

Exodus Through the Sinai Desert to the Reed Sea

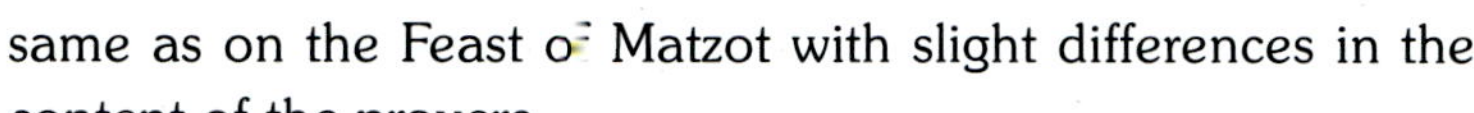

same as on the Feast of Matzot with slight differences in the content of the prayers.

The pilgrimage on Shavuot

On the Sunday, the fiftieth day of the Counting of the Omer, the Israelite-Samaritans make a pilgrimage to the top of Mount Gerizim. Buses bring pilgrims from Holon to Mount Gerizim at 2.00 a.m. to begin prayers for the pilgrimage. At 4.30 a.m., the pilgrims from Holon and Mount Gerizim go in song from the synagogue in Kiryat Luza to the top of Mount Gerizim, the locality of the sacred sites. The elderly go up in vehicles driven by Arabs from Nablus.

The three feasts of the year each last seven days. The Feast of Matzot lasts seven days including Passover, for on all the seven days one eats matzah. Shavuot and Succoth also each last seven days.

On the afternoon of Shavuot, the Israelite-Samaritan families receive the families of the priests in their homes, with tables laden with goodies and arak. The priests receive the families in turn. This is an old custom, observed even in the days when the community was poor and downcast. Its economic situation has greatly improved since then. On Shavuot, the Samaritan children enjoy themselves squirting water at passers-by.

The four great "times" of the seventh month
The seventh Rosh Hodesh, the "time" of the seventh month

On the seventh Rosh Hodesh, they blow the shofar and begin the ten days of Slihot (penitential prayers). The tenth is Yom Ha-Kippurim, the Day of Atonement.

At the end of morning prayers, the Israelite-Samaritans visit the priests who receive them at long tables laden with cakes, delicacies and drinks of various kinds. In the afternoon, the priests go to the people's homes. That day is the first of the ten days of Slihot, the most important of which is Yom Ha-Kippurim, the Day of Atonement. The Samaritan sages distinguish between the first nine days and the tenth, Yom Ha-Kippurim. They feel awe at the approach of the Day of Atonement.

On the ten days of Slihot, there are special prayers in the evening and in the morning. At the end of the service, they read the last two portions of the Torah.

The Sabbath between the "time" of the seventh month and Yom Kippur is called "the Sabbath of the ten days of Slihot," and there is a special morning prayer for forgiveness and God's mercy. When the "time" of the seventh month falls on a Sabbath, the following Sabbath will be "the Sabbath of the ten days of Slihot," and therefore the two last portions of the Torah are read before the "time" of the seventh month because there is no normal Sabbath between the four "times" of the seventh month: the "time" of the seventh month, Yom Ha-Kippurim, Succoth, and Shemini Atzeret.

Yom Ha-Kippurim = The Day of Atonement

This day falls on the tenth of the second month, on the second day. It is also called the "Day of Forgiveness and Mercy" or "the great Day of Atonement." There are many prayers and *piyyutim*. The whole Torah is read from one evening to the next. The shofar is blown at the beginning and end of the prayers. Everyone fasts. There is a light meal before the fast.

On the eve of Yom Ha-Kippurim, they visit the family graves. At the end of it, they begin to put up booths for Succoth.

The feast of Succoth (Tabernacles)

In the four days between Yom Ha-Kippurim and Succoth, they build the *succah* (booth) with four species: branches of citrus trees whose stems are strong enough to be used for the ceiling of the *succah*, date palm, laurel, and willow. Some of the booths are decorated with up to three hundred kilograms of fruit of various kinds. They sit there throughout the seven days but do not sleep there at night.

The *succah* is erected in the main room of the house. Until the sixth century CE, the *succah* was erected outside, but persecutions, fires and other factors led to a decision of the High

Blowing the Shofar
Photo: Ori Orhof

Priest to move it indoors. The Samaritans of Holon make the Mount Gerizim pilgrimage separately or in a group throughout the days of Succoth. When Succoth falls on a Sabbath, the Samaritans of Mount Gerizim make the pilgrimage on that day because of the closeness of their homes to the summit.

In the seven days of Succoth, a service is held in the evenings and mornings. Families visit each other. When visiting the *succah* of the High Priest, they bring the second symbolic tithe of the year. The first is brought by every man aged twenty or more on the day after the time of Passover, the second day of the seven days of the feast of Matzot. The *succah* is valid for religious purposes until the eve of Shemini Atzeret (the Eighth Day of Assembly).

The feast of the Third Pilgrimage

This begins at 2 a.m. There is a special prayer. The pilgrimage is the same as on the feasts of Matzot and Shavuot. At the end of it, they go home and sit in the *succah*.

Shemini Atzeret, the Eighth Day of Assembly

This day is called Shemini Atzeret in the Torah, and is the last of the Almighty's festivals according to tradition. It is the last "time" of the year. There is a long prayer-service, beginning at 1.00 a.m. and ending at 9.30 a.m. This is when the first fruits are brought to the High Priest in his *succah*. After prayers, the *succah* is taken down and the fruits distributed. Most of them are squeezed to make sweet pomegranate and lemon juice which is stored in a freezer to be drunk with cold water in the week of the feast of Matzot.

At the end of morning prayers, the priest circles the room of the synagogue with the Torah Scrolls, accompanied by the chanting of the congregation. After that, there are prayers for the repose of the dead.

On the Sabbath after Shemini Atzeret, they begin the reading of the first portion of the Book of Genesis.

The Samaritans celebrate only those holidays mentioned in the Torah. These are seven in all: Passover (Pesach), the Feast of Unleavened Bread, the Feast of Weeks (Shavuot), the First Day of the Seventh Month, the Day of Atonement (Yom Kippur), the Feast of Tabernacles (Succoth) and the Eighth Day of Assembly (Shemini Atzeret).

Unlike the Jews, their brethren within the people of Israel, the Samaritan Israelites do not celebrate Hannukah and Purim. Their New Year is celebrated fourteen days before Passover, and the eve of their Passover is marked by a sacrifice of sheep and male goats on Mount Gerizim.

11. Marqeh, a World-class Philosopher

The great wisdom of Marqeh, the greatest Israelite-Samaritan sage of all generations, is demonstrated in his marvellous works: in his poetry, *piyyutim*, and what remains of his expositions of the Torah, all of which testify to his wisdom and give him a place among the great philosophers of the world throughout the ages.

Underlying his belief in the "end of days," which represents a longing for a better world than this one, is the idea of the rediscovery of Moses' tabernacle, the first sanctuary of the people of Israel (*Exodus, chapter 8*) and the only one recognized by the Israelite-Samaritans, which according to their tradition was hidden from the people of Israel in a cave on Mount Gerizim two hundred and sixty years after their entry into the land of Canaan. The discovery will be made by the Taheb, a man from the tribe of Joseph who will be "a prophet like Moses." In order that all mankind should recognize him, he will have to manifest three signs: a jar of manna, Moses' rod, which is "the rod of the Lord," and the two cherubim. Some Samaritan-Israelite sages say: the jar of manna, Aaron's rod and the golden menorah, but the main question is not the nature of the signs used by "the prophet like Moses" to prove his identity, but when will it happen? What will indicate the transition from this world to the next one – a world of peace, prosperity and repose for all – without any need to die in order to reach that world of blessedness?

A belief in a change from a world full of tensions, wars, natural disasters and man-made disasters, in which nobody knows what tomorrow will bring, to another, more amenable world, full of happiness, without the ugliness of this one, exists in all faiths – in religions that believe in God and in those that believe in other earthly and heavenly entities. Until today, there have always been people, groups and religious movements which prophesied an "end of days," and when it did not happen at the time they foretold, found a reason to explain it in order to protect their livelihood. There were guileless people who sold all their possessions for a symbolic sum because they believed the prophecies of seers who not only announced the day but also the exact hour in which the next world would open its gates to all.

Such a belief exists in the three monotheistic religions today: Judaism, Christianity – which believes in the Father, his Son, and the Holy Spirit – and Islam, which believes in Allah. All three religions believe in the future appearance of a figure sent by God to bring believers to an incomparably better world than this one. Judaism believes in the "Messiah, son of David," Christianity in the second coming of Jesus the Messiah, and Islam in the appearance of the "Mahdi," but the appearance of the Messiah in all these religions – the Messiah who will bring his followers to the life of the world-to-come – is bound up with great suffering in this world. Judaism sees this great suffering, "the war of Gog and Magog," as "the birth pangs of the Messiah," birth pangs much greater and more painful than those experienced by a woman giving birth. The sufferings preceding redemption, the consequence of wars between humans, will lead to the coming of the Messiah. Nobody who has believed this has ever considered the illogic of thinking that only suffering can lead to redemption. If God promises believers a good and prosperous life, a life of peace on earth, why does he make it depend on such suffering, on the slaughter of hundreds of millions, or even billions of people? This illogic exists in both the Christian and Muslim religions. The Second Coming of Jesus, which appears to be needed because he did not fully realize his objectives on his First Coming, and the revelation of the "Mahdi" in Islam, are bound up with slaughter on a vast scale, greater than anything known until the present, when the heavenly hosts will also engage in the slaughter, and then the time will come at the end of all this when a new world will arise, better and cleaner than all this horror. When will the transitional period begin and when will it end, and when will the new world appear?

No member of these religions knows. There were also naïve Samaritan seers who told future generations that this would happen six thousand years after the creation of the world. They claimed that this is what they had heard from their predecessors. Although we are not so particular about the number of years that have passed since the creation and we are very particular about the number of years that have passed since our entry into the land promised to our fathers, it can be said that about five hundred years have now passed since the stated time.

Only Marqah knew the answer!

The rediscovery of Moses' tabernacle is the sign heralding the beginning of the better world and the move of all of us, living and dead, towards it.

Unlike the seers of other religions, Marqah knew very well when it would happen. In a stanza of his *piyyut* "Let us praise," which is chanted on every second Sabbath in the month and on festivals and their Sabbaths, he wrote: "The good and mighty God declares that the tabernacle will be revealed not in wars, not in killing and slaughter, but when there is an improvement in the moral conduct of the children of Israel as an example to all humanity, and the hearts of the children of Israel will be united, and their hearts and speech will be filled with the awe of God. That is what God asks." Then the tabernacle of Moses will be revealed as a cardinal sign of the transition to a better world. It is the quality of hearts and speech at the same moral level that will bring it about.

After the change to a better world, the resurrection of the dead will take place. This also applies to the members of other religions – Jews, Christians and Muslims – who will recognise the truth of the Israelite-Samaritan teachings. All will stand before God, Moses and the Torah. Those whose sins, such as murder and adultery, have condemned them to death in the Torah, will not be resurrected. The other sinners will receive absolution through the prayers of Moses and will go to heaven where the fathers of the Israelite people already dwell, and which is the world of the sacred line: Abraham, Isaac, Jacob, Joseph, Moses, Aaron, Eliezer, Itamar and Pinhas. Those whose sins are not absolved will be sentenced to descend to the netherworld (sheol).

Samaritan clock poster for the Day of Atonement
Photo: Ori Orhof

12. The Customs of Purity and Impurity

Everyday life

In the everyday life of the Israelite-Samaritans, in the present as in the past, the commandments concerning menstruation are scrupulously observed, although the punishment for those who do not keep them is not clear in the written Torah. The matter involves the purity of the family and also the structure of the family. When there is no female neighbor fulfilling the duties of the mother of the house as a housewife, the husband may fulfill those duties in the seven monthly days of menstruation, and in addition to his normal work he will be the mother of the house. The husband will clean, wash the dishes, do the laundry, cook, serve, change the children's diapers, dress the children and take them to the kindergarten or elementary school - all this while his wife is resting in her room or out of the home in her job or studying or engaging in social activities.

In everyday life the Israelite-Samaritans insist on observing the words of the Torah according to their literal interpretation. The customs encourage good relationships between neighbors. A female neighbor takes care of the children of the woman during the 41 days of separation between her and her husband after the birth of a boy or 80 days of separation after the birth of a girl due to the fact that the separation prohibits any touching. Then the woman does the same for her female neighbor after the neighbor gives birth.

It also strengthens the relationship between husband and wife that the husband becomes aware of his wife's duties in

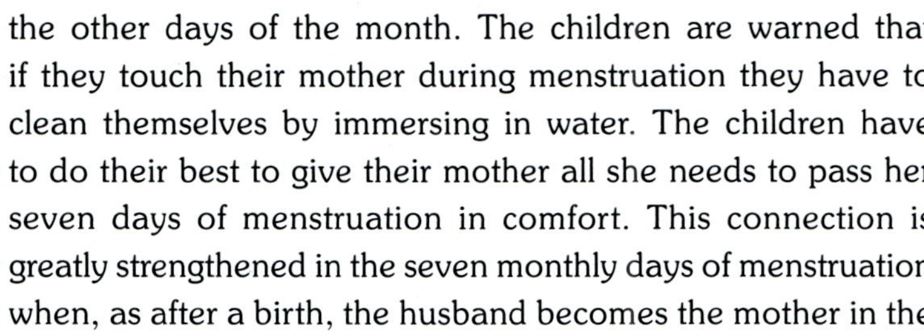

the other days of the month. The children are warned that if they touch their mother during menstruation they have to clean themselves by immersing in water. The children have to do their best to give their mother all she needs to pass her seven days of menstruation in comfort. This connection is greatly strengthened in the seven monthly days of menstruation when, as after a birth, the husband becomes the mother in the house.

Past and present

In recent generations houses have replaced tents and all the modern facilities ensuring hot water for drinking, washing and washing up are provided.

In place of the separate tent where the menstruating women lived in the 7, 41, and 80 days of menstruation, they have a special room in the house or apartment, furnished like a room in a hotel with a separate toilet. The public bath in the yard between the tents or houses that existed before the modern facilities were installed has been replaced by a private bath.

The woman fills the bath or the jacuzzi with warm water, and then she turns on the tap and removes the plug at the bottom of the bath to ensure hot running water.

Then she immerses her naked body in the hot water from head to feet. Her clothes are immersed in water before her own immersion and she is helped by her neighbor, husband or children who remove them from the bath. The clothes are later taken to a laundry by the woman herself. This process is repeated after 7, 41 or 80 days. On the other days of menstruation a daily shower is taken with no need for immersion in the bath.

On the happy occasion of circumcision, on the eighth day after the birth of a boy, if the family wants the boy to be circumcised in a pure state, they must immerse him in warm water before the circumcision ceremony and give him back to his impure mother after the ceremony is over.

Complete separation without touching

These commandments are living commandments. The separation between husband and wife for 7, 41 or 80 days is complete and strengthens the structure of the family. It must therefore be observed at all times to support the wholeness of the entire congregation.

During her period of menstruation the woman should not touch anything that moves, any person or any tool. There is a complete separation between her and the other members of the community. The members of her household must give her all she needs in food and clothes and anything she asks for without touching. They put it down and she takes it. In the present as in the past, anything that she touches becomes impure and must be immersed in water, and if that is not possible, as in the case of the bed she uses, it must be cleansed by fire. She immerses any utensils she uses for her food in boiling water. At the end of the period of menstruation, she immerses in water all the utensils she used during the period: plates, cups, knives, spoons and forks. They are all immersed in boiling water in the bathroom washbasin.

The garbage she accumulates during the period is collected and thrown by her in a public bin, preferably in a different neighborhood.

Chairs and tables are rinsed in water and kept in the yard during the night until dawn. Books and electrical appliances are not impure. After the woman places them in a neutral area, a pure person can take them. The same applies to portable computers, home computers, and mobile phones.

Resuming contact between husband and wife

After the immersion, the woman, married or unmarried, wears fresh clothes and returns to the family circle, embraced by her family members. If someone touches her during the day in the time of menstruation, the person is impure and is separated for seven days. Sexual relations between husband and wife after immersion at the end of the period are encouraged.

When a boy is born, for the first 14 days she has to devote

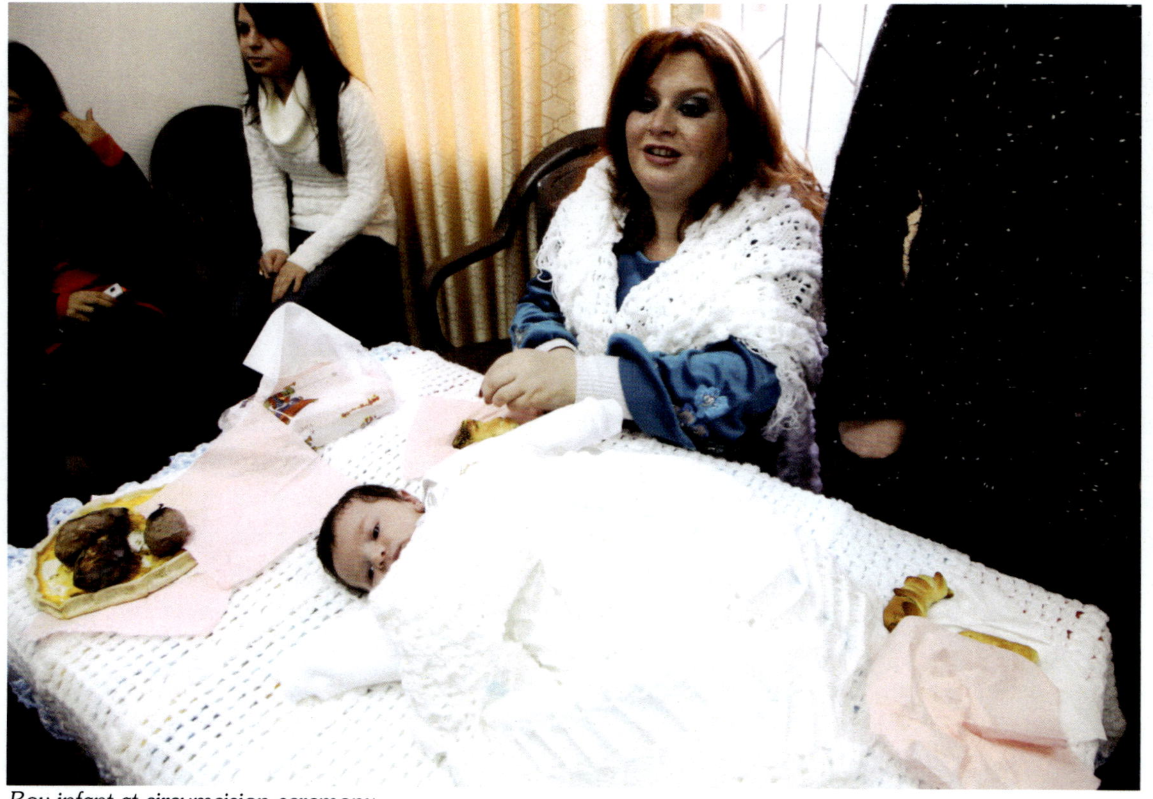

Boy infant at circumcision ceremony
Photo: Ori Orhof

Celebrating the Brit Milah
Photo: Ori Orhof

herself entirely to the newborn. Any person who touches her must be immersed in water and be impure for seven days. During the other days: 27 after the birth of a boy and 66 after the birth of a girl, she can go out, but keep herself from touching anyone else apart from another impure woman like herself.

This separation and the way the husband and children treat the woman during her period make the chances of divorce almost zero.

It is recommended for a woman during her period to find other women having their period and go out with them to shows or the theater in order not to trouble her family taking care of maintaining the house or apartment.

It is recommended for a husband to speak especially lovingly to his wife during the days of separation. It will calm her and make it easier for her to cope with her condition.

As menstruation usually does not happen suddenly, it is recommended for a woman to prepare all she needs, clothes, diapers, etc, for the time of her period.

On Friday evenings and Saturdays, she eats at a separate table close to her family that prepares the table and food for her before she sits down. Then she collects all the utensils, washing them and immersing them in boiling water in the bathroom washbasin.

Wall-to-wall carpets are considered part of the floor. Movable carpets or rags that she touches during her period are immersed in water. Bedclothes are cleansed by singeing them with burning paper. It is recommended that after the 41 or 80 days of separation, the husband takes his wife on a new honeymoon to compensate them for the long days of separation and in order to satisfy their spiritual and sexual needs. Love reaches a climax during these honeymoons.

A girl from outside of the community who marries an Israelite-Samaritan groom generally gains a loving husband who cares for their children and is devoted to her and the family.

Unfaithfulness on the part of one member of the couple can cause the person to leave his/her spouse and the community if there are two or three witnesses to the infidelity before the High Priest.

Male menstruation

Reasons: a wet dream, or sexual relations between husband and wife causes ejaculation of seed.

On an ordinary day the wife and her husband wash themselves with water and stay impure until the evening. Anyone who touches a grave, washes the dead or carries the dead to his grave and buries him, must immerse himself in a bath and stay impure till the evening, following a decision taken by the High Priests in the 19th century.

On Friday evening, sexual relations are forbidden, because a man should keep himself clean, and ejaculation would make him impure during the Sabbath. In the case of a wet dream or uncontrolled ejaculation, a man must wash himself and be impure until the evening.

In the synagogue, after washing himself, a man of any age must sit at the back and is not allowed to raise his voice or hold a Torah or prayer book. It is not a disgrace as it happens to everybody. He cannot participate in the reading of the weekly portion of the Torah.

In his times of impurity, a ritual slaughterer does not count as a slaughterer, because he normally slaughters in the direction of Mount Gerizim and speaks words of Torah.

13. Four Clans

The head of the Samaritan Israelite community is the High Priest, who is also head of the Ha'Abta'ee priestly clan, descendants of **Aaron**, brother of Moses, through his son, Itamar. The three other Samaritan clans descend from the sons of Joseph: the Tsedaka Hatsafari from the **Tribe of Manasseh**, and the Danfi [Altif + Hassetari (Sassoni)] and the Marchivi [Marchiv + Yehoshua] from the **Tribe of Ephraim**.

The Territories of the Tribes of Israel

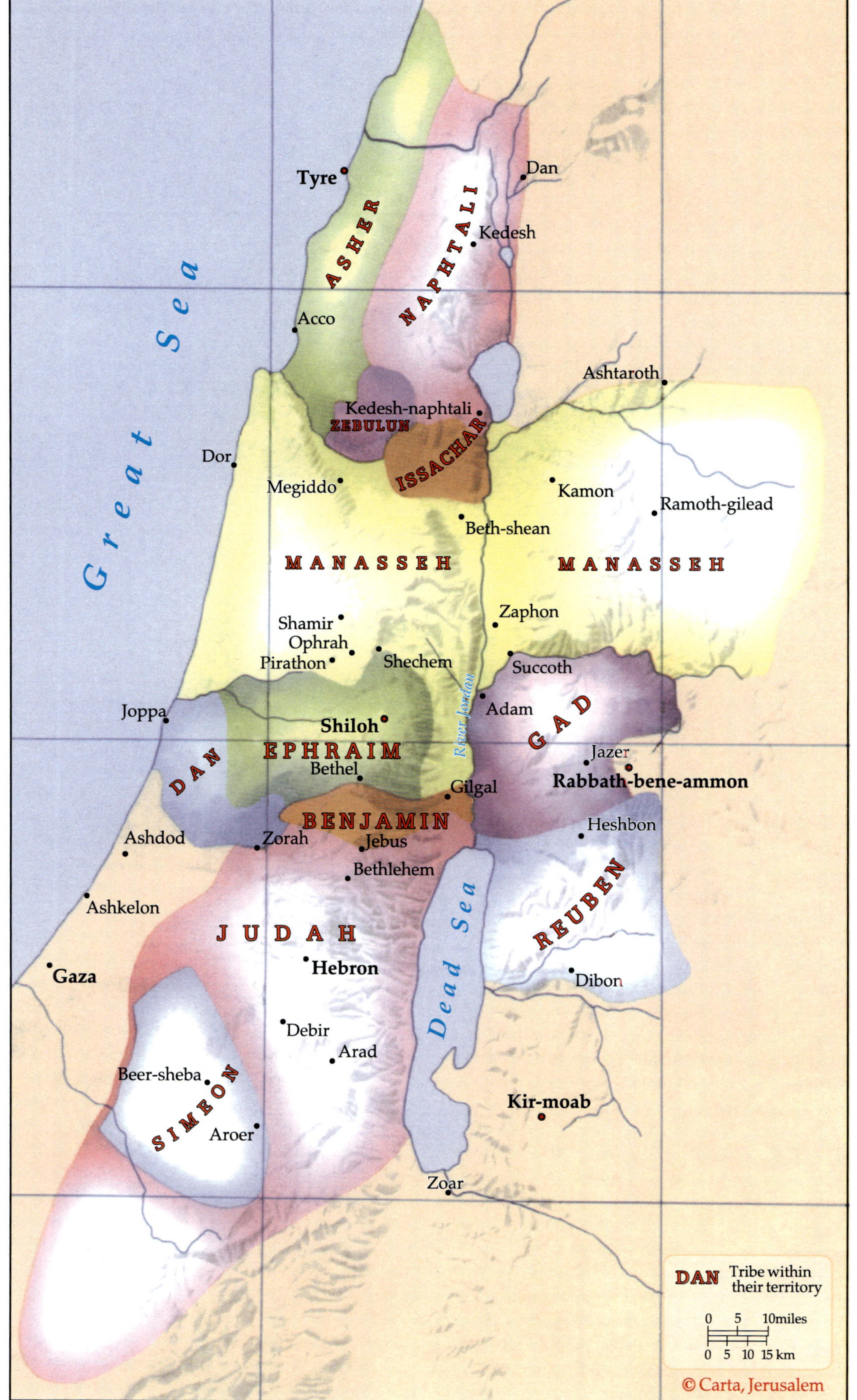

14. Samaritan Centers

Samaritan life is concentrated in two centers. Nearly half the community lives in the Kiryat Luza neighborhood on Mt. Gerizim throughout the year. Most of the other half of the community resides in the Samaritan neighborhood in Holon, which was established in 1954-55. The community is grateful for the efforts of its late leader, Yefet b. Avraham Tsedaka Hatsafari, of blessed memory, and the great assistance of the second President of the State of Israel, the late Yitzhak Ben-Zvi, of blessed memory, as well as the mayors of Holon, the late Haim Kugel, and the late Pinhas Eilon, of blessed memory, who allotted the land for the neighborhood and helped to obtain the requisite financial assistance.

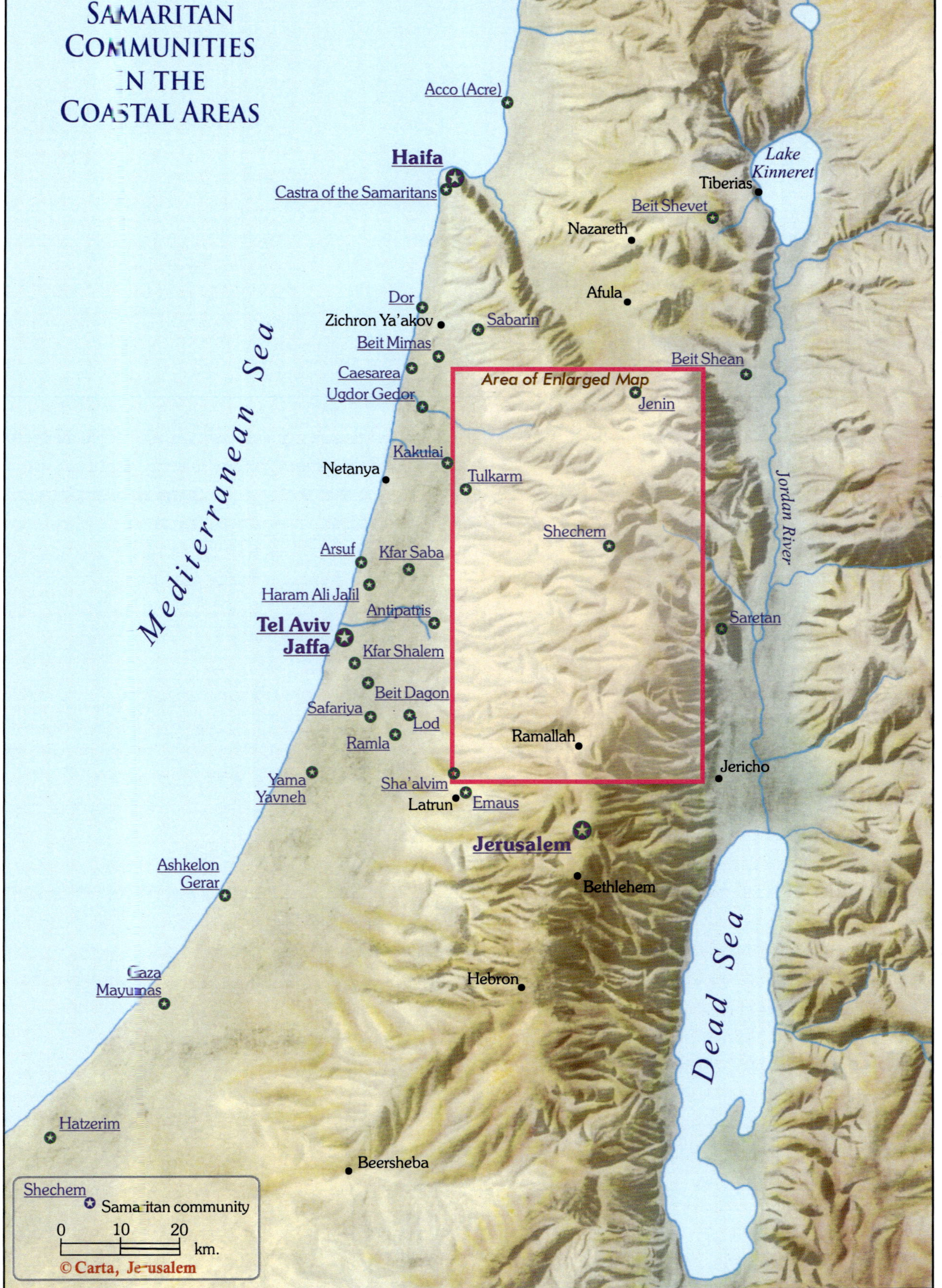

Samaritan Communities in the Samarian Mountains

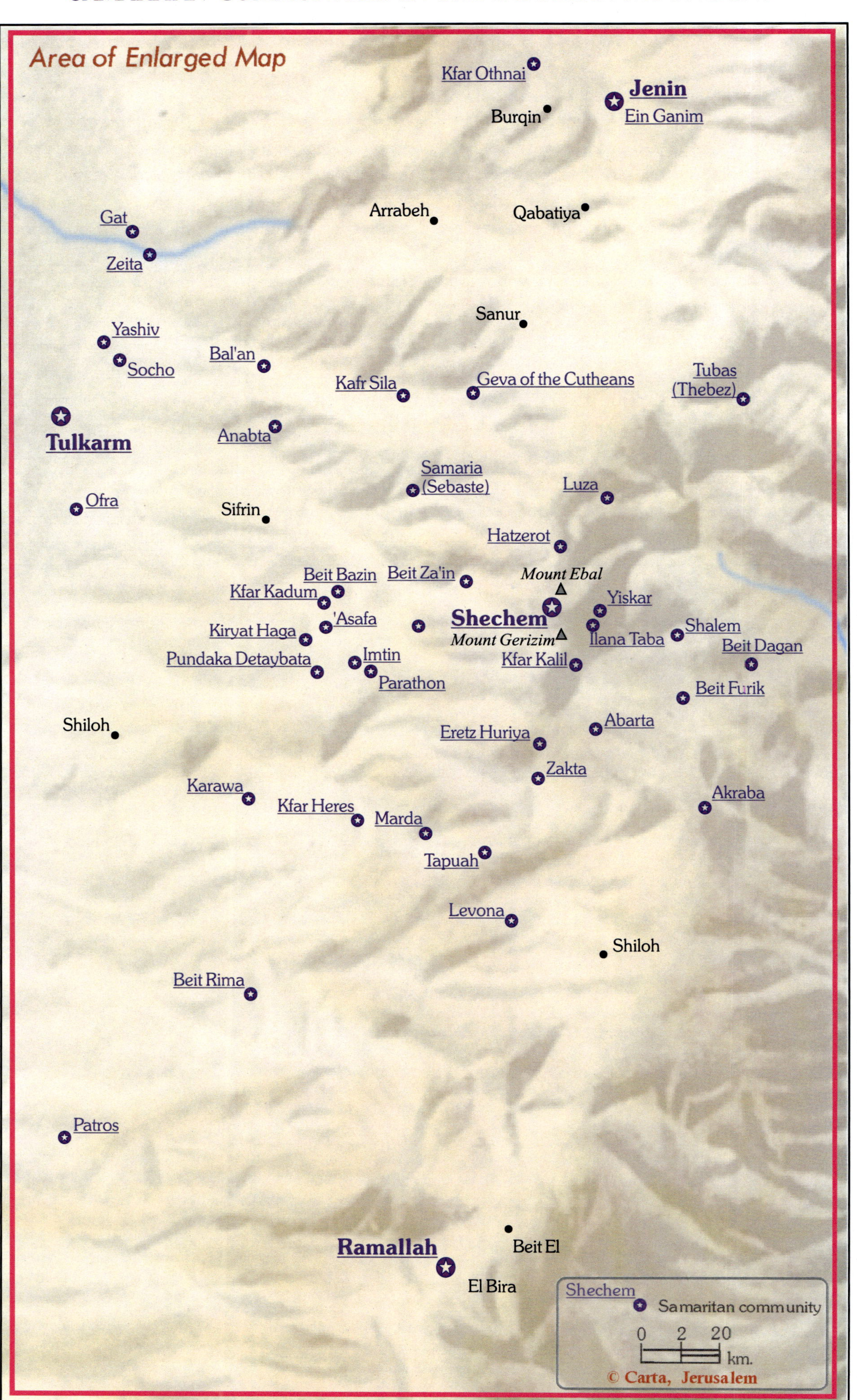

15. Politics

Due to the peace process between the government of Israel and the Palestinians, the community has been split, in terms of the areas under their control, since the end of 1995. Public affairs, particularly concerning improvement of the quality of life in both centers, are conducted by committees in Holon for predetermined periods and in Kiryat Luza in accordance with the instructions of the High Priest. The growth of the community in the last generation necessitates the expansion of the residential and living areas of the two centers and possibly the planning of a third center.

At Kiryat Luza, rapid construction to expand the neighborhood is taking place in response to the needs of the younger generation. The Israelite-Samaritans have established an International Peace Center on Mount Gerizim as a place for peace seekers from all over the world to meet conflicting groups, and especially those involved in the Palestinian-Israeli confrontation. Senior officials of both sides are very much in favor of the idea.

In general, the Israelite-Samaritans are not officially involved in the politics of the region, and by emphasizing their ancient heritage and their uniqueness as one of the oldest groups in the civilized world, they wish to act as a bridge of peace between entities in conflict in the Middle East and provide a modest contribution to making peace. Their neutral attitude and their friendship with all parties in the Middle East has helped them to be the only entity in the Middle East fully respected by all sides in the politics of the region.

16. Culture and Education

There is an active educational and cultural life in the Samaritan community on a number of levels: there are cultural activities, summer day camps, exhibitions, and community centers which operate mainly in the spring and summer and offer courses and classes of enrichment. There are also schools which teach the Samaritan tradition, operating from Sunday to Thursday, in the afternoon.

In 1969, the brothers Benyamim and Yefet ben Ratson Tsedaka established A.B.–The Samaritan News, the first Samaritan newspaper, generally published on a biweekly basis in four languages, all appearing in the same edition: ancient Hebrew, modern Hebrew, Arabic and English. In 1981, the editors of A.B. established the A.B. Institute of Samaritan Studies, named after the late Yefet ben Abraham Tsedaka, the

Byzantine Church of the 6th century CE and Moslem grave of the 12th century CE on Mount Gerizim
Image taken as part of the Elef Millim project trip to Mount Gerizim
Source: Own work; Author : Deror_avi
Via Wikimedia Commons

head of the Samaritan community in Israel. [His leadership years: 1928-1982.] The institute serves as a focal point for scholars and university students. They receive instruction and guidance at the institute for the research they conduct in Samaritan studies. In Kiryat Luza there are three other institutions which provide information about the Samaritans to visitors and the Arab neighbors. The main Web site – a center of correct information about Israelite-Samaritans is: israelite-samaritans.com

In the winter months, there is extensive activity in the community, which copies and prepares Torahs and prayer books for publication, some of which are published in limited editions. On Mount Gerizim there is an interesting Visitors' Center with all the main artifacts of the Israelite heritage, run by the committee.

On the crest of the mountain, there is a highly organized and developed Mount Gerizim National Garden containing the Holy Sites of the Israelite-Samaritans and the archaeological site of the ancient city of Luza in the 6th-2nd centuries BCE. There is also a reconstructed Byzantine Church of the 6th century CE and a Moslem grave of the 12th century CE. They are all under the management of the Israel Nature and Parks Authority.

17. Samaritan Studies

The science of Samaritan studies has developed very rapidly since the establishment of the Society of Samaritan Studies in Paris in October 1985. Since then, the society has helped to organize many International conferences of Samaritan Studies, the first of which was held in Tel Aviv, Israel in 1998. The proceedings of these conferences contain the full texts of all lectures on various subjects which cast light on the different aspects of Samaritan Studies. Between congresses there are conferences of the Society of Biblical Literature (SBL) and the European Association of Biblical Studies (EABS) that devote sessions to Samaritan Studies.

18. Israelite-Samaritan Music

Samaritan music is solely vocal, unaccompanied by instruments, handed down during the hundred and thirty generations of the existence of the ancient Israelite-Samaritan people in the land of Israel. It has been passed on in two ways:

a. Through formal study: every Samaritan boy or girl studies for about an hour a day with Samaritan teachers at the Community Center when they come home from school. They learn reading, liturgy and poetry in ancient Hebrew and in the Aramaic dialect still used today by the Samaritans.

b. By participation in prayer services at the Samaritan synagogue on every Sabbath and festival.

Thus the musical tradition is preserved, with its thousands of different songs and melodies, some of which are sung in prayer services and secular ceremonies, on Sabbath and festivals and

Scene from the Opera "Samaritans" by Yuval Avital, Milan, Italy, 2010
Performance by the choir of Israelite-Samaritan ancient music.
Photo: Ori Orhof

on joyous as well as sorrowful occasions.

Some of the songs have been handed down directly – a clear echo of ancient Israelite song; some were written by Samaritan composers in the latter half of the first millennium and some in the first half of the second millennium of the modern era. There is an active choir of Israelite-Samaritan music performing regularly on world stages in New York, Paris, Berlin, London, Tokyo, Italy and Spain. The choir is run by the A.B.– Institute of Samaritan Studies.

Stained glass window of the south side aisle of the Cathedral of Notre Dame of Chatres; panel 044 showing the parable of the Good Samaritan
Source: Own work
Author:MOSSOT
Via Wikimedia Commons

19. The Youth

Serious efforts have been made to encourage the younger generation to become involved in the internal affairs of the community. Kiryat Luza reestablished a youth club in 1982, with about 150 members, that organizes sports activities and a basketball team, hiking trips and courses in the fall and winter months for the study of their heritage. The same activities with similar numbers take place in Holon.

The Good Samaritan
By Vincent van Gogh (1853–1890)
Saint-Rémy, May 1890
Current location: Kröller-Müller Museum
Source/Photographer: repro from artbook
Via Wikimedia Commons